Bible Studies

Job
Ecclesiastes

Second Edition

James Malm

ISBN 978-1-989208-08-3

Copyright 2018
James Malm
All rights reserved

Unless otherwise noted all scriptures
are quoted from the King James Version

Dedication

*This work is dedicated to the Great God
whose house is eternity; the Father and Sovereign of all that exists and
the sum of all Truth, Wisdom, Love, Justice and Mercy.
May God's house be filled with children whose chief joy
is to be like Him!*

Visit Our Website
theshininglight.info

Table of Contents

Job 7

    Introduction 8
    Job 1 11
    Job 2 15
    Job 3 18
    Job 4 20
    Job 5 22
    Job 6 25
    Job 7 28
    Job 8 31
    Job 9 34
    Job 10 38
    Job 11 40
    Job 12 42
    Job 13 44
    Job 14 47
    Job 15 51
    Job 16 54
    Job 17 57
    Job 18 61
    Job 19 63
    Job 20 71
    Job 21 76
    Job 22 79
    Job 23 82
    Job 24 84
    Job 25 87
    Job 26 88
    Job 27 90
    Job 28 92
    Job 29 95
    Job 30 98

Job 31	101
Job 32	106
Job 33	109
Job 34	112
Job 35	118
Job 36	120
Job 37	124
The Great Sin of Today's Spiritual Ekklesia	127
Job 38	141
The Unicorn	145
Job 39	148
Job 40	150
Job 41	153
Job 42	156
Ecclesiastes	**161**
Introduction	162
Ecclesiastes 1	169
Ecclesiastes 2	172
Ecclesiastes 3	176
Ecclesiastes 4	179
Ecclesiastes 5	182
Ecclesiastes 6	185
Ecclesiastes 7	187
Ecclesiastes 8	192
Ecclesiastes 9	196
Ecclesiastes 10	199
Ecclesiastes 11	203
Ecclesiastes 12	206

Job

Introduction

The Book of Job is close to Ecclesiastes in its format of reasoning about the higher questions of life. Why does a loving God allow suffering? Why does God allow the righteous to suffer and many wicked to prosper? Since both the wicked and the righteous die: Is this physical existence and universal physical death, all there is to life?

In the broader picture, Job is an example of the patient loyalty to God of a righteous man, during intense trials. Job knows that God could deliver him and remains loyal and faithful to God throughout his testing; absolutely loyal to God in spite of his personal sufferings. But Job does has an unnoticed problem; he continually defends his own integrity, justifying himself.

The book of Job is also filled with messages about humility before God, the transitory nature of physical things and the Greatness and Glory of God.

The name Job (pron.: /ˈdʒoʊb/; Hebrew: אִיּוֹב ʾiyobh), commonly referred to in English as Job. The English is from 'Iyowb, or ē·yōve' and in Arabic Ayyub, and **more properly pronounced in English as "ee-yob"**, the letter "J" being a relatively modern invention should not properly be applied to this ancient word.

Job means "hated"

Like most Old Testament books, Job was originally written in Hebrew. And like the Psalms, Proverbs, the Song of Solomon, Ecclesiastes, and large portions of the prophetic books, Job is poetry.

Most people today think of poetry in terms of rhythm and rhyme.

Hebrew verse, however, consists of a balance of thoughts more than of words and sounds. Such balance is called parallelism. This means that one line in Hebrew poetry parallels the next. The second part of a verse echoes the idea of the first, contrasts with it, or expands on it. The following are some illustrations of parallelism in Job.

Here Job wishes he had never been born:

>Part One: "MAY THE DAY OF MY BIRTH PERISH,"
>
>Part Two echoes back with: "AND THE NIGHT IT WAS SAID, A BOY IS BORN!" (Job 3:3)
>
>Another example:
>
>Part One: "*Is not your wickedness great?*"
>
>Part Two: "*Are not your sins endless?*" (Job 22:5)

The point of Ecclesiastes and Job is that God is far greater than man, and God works according to his own purposes and not man's for the purpose of the ultimate good of his creation and that sometimes even good men must suffer for the greater good, as they and others are molded into what God has ordained for each one: And that there is indeed far more to life than mere physical life ending with the grave, as the concepts of salvation from death and the eternal life are introduced.

Job lived about 2,000 BC, just after the days of Abraham. Job is described as living in the land of Buz which later became a part of Edom just south of the Dead Sea and was a friend and member of the immediate children of Esau who were famous for their wisdom at that time. This puts Job as living during the time of Jacob.

Bildad, son of Shuach [Also called Shuach, was the sixth and last of **Keturah's sons** [by Abraham] has a name meaning *wealth* (Strong: SHD 7744). He was the progenitor of the Shuhites, the most notable of whom was **Bildad, son of Shuach**, and one of Job's 'comforters' (Job 2:11).

The biblical account of Job records another interesting proof of Job.

Another of Job's friends is mentioned in Job 2:11 Now when Job's three friends heard of all this evil that was come upon him, they came every one from his own place; **Eliphaz the Temanite**

This Eliphaz was the duke Timnah, Gen 36:40]: —This Eliphaz [Timnah] is the first son of Esau! Eliphaz [Timnah] dwelled in a village of Mount Seir and named his land and his son Temen after himself.

Genesis 36:8 Thus dwelt Esau in mount Seir: Esau is Edom. **36:9** And these are the generations of Esau the father of the Edomites in mount Seir: **36:10** These are the names of Esau's sons; **Eliphaz** [also called Timnah Gen 36:40] the son of Adah the wife of Esau, Reuel the son of Bashemath the wife of Esau.

Eliphaz [Timnah] was the firstborn son of Esau; and Shuach, the sixth and last of Keturah's sons by Abraham was the father of Bildad. Two of Job's friends being son's of Esau would date Job to the era of the sons of Esau.

Mount Seir was named for Seir, the Horite, whose offspring had inhabited the area (Genesis 14:6, 36:20) until the children of Esau (the Edomites) moved into the area and gradually absorbed or assimilated the Horites and took possession of the city (Deuteronomy 2:4-5, 12, 22).

From that time Mount Seir has become synonymous with Esau who took possession of Seir and the Horites living there. (Genesis 32:3; 33:14, 16; 36:8; Joshua 24:4).

Job is described in a Syriac text as living in the land of Ausis, on the borders of Idumea and Arabia: and his name was Jobab; and having taken an Arabian wife, he begot a son whose name was Ennon.

Job [Eyov] was the son of Zare, one of the sons of Esau, and of his mother Bosorrha.

It appears that Job was a ruler or great man of Esau in the area of Mount Seir and that his three friends were his close advisers, all of whom were the son's of Esau

Noah, Daniel, and Job are presented in scripture as some of the most righteous and wisest men who have even lived.

God calls Job "perfect" before him, just as God said that Noah was "perfect" during the generations in which he lived. God inspired Ezekiel to write of the now soon coming great tribulation like this.

Ezekiel 14:20 Though **Noah, Daniel, and Job** were in it, as I live, saith the Lord GOD, they shall deliver neither son nor daughter; they shall but deliver their own souls by their righteousness.

Job 1

This is a third person account of the testing of Job.

Job 1:1 There was a man in the land of Uz, whose name was Job; and that man **was perfect and upright, and one that feared God, and eschewed evil**.

1:2 And there were born unto him seven sons and three daughters. **1:3** His substance also was seven thousand sheep, and three thousand camels, and five hundred yoke of oxen, and five hundred she asses, and a very great household; so that this man was the greatest of all the men of the east.

1:4 And his sons went and feasted in their houses, every one his day [they took turns partying EVERY DAY; this has NOTHING to do with birthdays]; and sent and called for their three sisters to eat and to drink with them.

When his children were feasting, Job feared that in a drunken state they might do some evil deed; and so Job prayed for and made offerings for his children. Job's offerings were continual which means the feasting was continual.

1:5 And it was so, when the days of their feasting were gone about, that Job sent and sanctified them, and rose up early in the morning, and offered burnt offerings according to the number of them all: for Job said, It may be that my sons have sinned, and cursed God in their hearts. **Thus did Job continually.**

The sons of God here were angels and were sons by virtue of having been created by God. This refers to spirit angelic beings, since flesh cannot cross the expanse between the earth and God's throne.

1:6 Now there was a day when the sons of God came to present themselves before the LORD [YHVH], and Satan came also among them.

Satan was restricted to the earth after his rebellion but still had access to his Warden. God the Father would have denied contact to Satan the originator of rebellion and sin and this "God" was certainly the Being who later gave up his godhood to become flesh as Jesus Christ. He asks the Adversary where he has been and what he has been doing and Satan is evasive.

1:7 And the LORD said unto Satan, Whence comest thou? Then Satan answered the LORD, and said, From going to and fro in the earth, and from walking up and down in it.

God then asks Satan about Job, clearly intending to bring Job to Satan's attention for God's own purpose. What follows is not only a lesson for Job, it is a lesson for all who read this story and it was a lesson for Satan himself.

1:8 And the LORD said unto Satan, Hast thou considered my servant Job, that there is none like him in the earth, a perfect and an upright man, one that feareth God, and escheweth evil?

Satan responds to God's praise of Job with the accusation that Job is faithful to God only for a reward. This accusation by Satan is very true of very many religions people today, who are merely going through the motions of what they think is necessary to gain a reward from God.

One of the many lessons of Job is that we as the espoused bride, are to be faithful in BOTH good times and bad; whether being blessed and or suffering.

Job is a lesson that God the Almighty is sovereign and does as he wills, which is for the good of his people. Often there is a greater good in experiencing various things, than there is in some immediate blessing.

Trials teach us; patience, faith, perseverance, humility, wisdom and empathy for others and help us to understand the transitory nature and weakness of the flesh, and our need for God's deliverance.

Job is also an allegory of the converted life; those who endure all things in this life to obey and please God may still suffer but they will have their reward in the future.

All the things that we lose or give up for zeal to God; will be replaced and far more at the appointed time.

> **Matthew 19:28** And Jesus said unto them, Verily I say unto you, That ye which have followed me, in the regeneration when the Son of man shall sit in the throne of his glory, ye also shall sit upon twelve thrones, judging the twelve tribes of Israel.
>
> **19:29** And every one that hath forsaken houses, or brethren, or sisters, or father, or mother, or wife, or children, or lands, for my name's sake, shall receive an hundredfold, and shall inherit everlasting life.

Job 1:9 Then Satan answered the LORD, and said, Doth Job fear God for nought? **1:10** Hast not thou made an hedge about him, and about his house, and about all that he hath on every side? thou hast blessed the work of his hands, and his substance is increased in the land.

Satan then challenges God to prove Job's faithfulness by taking away his blessings right down to his health.

It is VERY important to understand that when we are zealous and faithful for God and his commandments; we WILL be persecuted by Satan. This account demonstrates that Satan can do NOTHING unless God permits it, and God permits only what he knows is for our ultimate good.

God allows trials to test and build stronger character in his people. A lack of physical blessings does not mean that God is not working with us. See Hebrews 11.

1:11 But put forth thine hand now, and touch all that he hath, and he will curse thee to thy face.

God gives Satan permission to test Job and Satan removes all of Job's wealth and blessings including his ten children.

Consider this man's love for his children that he made sacrifice and gave his substance just in case they MIGHT have possibly sinned. Consider the agony of spirit that must have fallen on Job who did not know about this heavenly conversation and this came as a complete surprise and overwhelming shock.

As a parent, I weep for Job in these sufferings; yet God allowed a righteous man to suffer so that he might be further perfected.

John 15:1 I am the true vine, and my Father is the husbandman. **15:2** Every branch in me that beareth not fruit he taketh away: and **every branch that beareth fruit, he purgeth it, that it may bring forth more fruit.**

Job 1:12 And the LORD said unto Satan, Behold, all that he hath is in thy power; only upon himself put not forth thine hand. So Satan went forth from the presence of the LORD.

1:13 And there was a day when his sons and his daughters were eating and drinking wine in their eldest brother's house: **1:14** And there came a messenger unto Job, and said, The oxen were plowing, and the asses feeding beside them: **1:15** And the Sabeans fell upon them, and took them away; yea, they have slain the servants with the edge of the sword; and I only am escaped alone to tell thee.

1:16 While he was yet speaking, there came also another, and said, The fire of God is fallen from heaven, and hath burned up the sheep, and the servants, and consumed them; and I only am escaped alone to tell thee.

1:17 While he was yet speaking, there came also another, and said, The Chaldeans made out three bands, and fell upon the camels, and have carried them away, yea, and slain the servants with the edge of the sword; and I only am escaped alone to tell thee.

1:18 While he was yet speaking, there came also another, and said, Thy sons and thy daughters were eating and drinking wine in their eldest brother's house: **1:19** And, behold, there came a great wind from the wilderness, and smote the four corners of the house, and it fell upon the young men, and they are dead; and I only am escaped alone to tell thee.

Who among us has this attitude of Job?

1:20 Then Job arose, and rent his mantle, and shaved his head, and fell down upon the ground, and worshipped, **1:21 And said, Naked came I out of my mother's womb, and naked shall I return thither: the LORD gave, and the LORD hath taken away; blessed be the name of the LORD.**

In his hour of trial, Job mourned and sought out the Eternal and was absolutely faithful.

1:22 In all this Job sinned not, nor charged God foolishly.

Now the angels and Satan appeared before God to give an account of their activities, and God inquires of Satan, only to have Satan evade the question.

Job 2

Job 2:1 Again there was a day when the sons of God came to present themselves before the LORD, and Satan came also among them to present himself before the LORD.

2:2 And the LORD said unto Satan, From whence comest thou? And Satan answered the LORD, and said, From going to and fro in the earth, and from walking up and down in it.

God then asks Satan about Job's loyalty to God in spite of his trials. Here God admits that this trial of Job was without cause, yet there was a godly purpose which Satan did not comprehend.

2:3 And the LORD said unto Satan, Hast thou considered my servant Job, that there is none like him in the earth, a perfect and an upright man, one that feareth God, and escheweth evil? and still he holdeth fast his integrity, although thou movedst me against him, **to destroy him without cause**.

Satan responds, saying that Job is loyal for fear of his life.

Let me ask this also: How many of the brethren are loyal to a corporate church organization out of FEAR that leaving their group will cut them off from God and eternal life?

The exact opposite is the truth; exalting an organization of men and their false traditions cuts one off from God. Only by NOT idolizing men and traditions, only by being absolutely faithful and zealous to live by every Word of God will we become and remain reconciled to God!

2:4 And Satan answered the LORD, and said, Skin for skin, yea, all that a man hath will he give for his life.

2:5 But put forth thine hand now, and touch his bone and his flesh, and he will curse thee to thy face.

God then gives Satan full authority to strike Job with plagues.

2:6 And the LORD said unto Satan, Behold, he is in thine hand; but save his life.

Satan then strikes Job with painful boils over his entire body. A boil is a large swelling puss filled very painful eruption; and Job takes a potsherd to scrape away the puss and to try and ease his pain by applying pressure.

2:7 So went Satan forth from the presence of the LORD, and smote Job with sore boils from the sole of his foot unto his crown. **2:8** And he took him a potsherd to scrape himself withal; and he sat down among the ashes.

In his great distress his wife advises him to blame God for his suffering and seek death. After all it does seem that God was being unjust and trying Job for no reason apparent to the couple.

The lesson here is that when we are in trials we must not blame God for supposedly bringing a trial without a reason. We must patiently ask God to reveal to us the reasons for the trial and ask him to teach us the things that God wants us to learn from the situation.

2:9 Then said his wife unto him, Dost thou still retain thine integrity? curse God, and die.

Yet Job remained faithful and zealous for God and rebuked his wife, insisting that man must submit to God in good and bad times.

2:10 But he said unto her, Thou speakest as one of the foolish women speaketh. **What? shall we receive good at the hand of God, and shall we not receive evil? In all this did not Job sin with his lips.**

Now the three friends of Job met with him to comfort him and to try and help him.

2:11 Now when Job's three friends heard of all this evil that was come upon him, they came every one from his own place; Eliphaz the Temanite, and Bildad the Shuhite, and Zophar the Naamathite: for they had made an appointment together to come to mourn with him and to comfort him.

For seven days and nights they mourned with Job, speechless at his affliction; thinking perhaps about the possible reasons for so great a suffering, so as to advise and help their good friend.

2:12 And when they lifted up their eyes afar off, and knew him not, they lifted up their voice, and wept; and they rent every one his mantle, and sprinkled dust upon their heads toward heaven. **2:13** So they sat down with him upon the ground seven days and seven nights, and none spake a word unto him: for they saw that his grief was very great.

Job 3

A complex discussion now begins which contains many truths and errors by the various participants.

Job speaks out in his agony and curses his life for all its sorrows and suffering; saying that is would be better to never have lived than to experience such sufferings. He asks the question; Why live at all, if it holds such agonies?

Job 3:1 After this opened Job his mouth, and cursed his day.

3:2 And Job spake, and said, **3:3** Let the day perish wherein I was born, and the night in which it was said, There is a man child conceived. **3:4** Let that day be darkness; let not God regard it from above, neither let the light shine upon it. **3:5** Let darkness and the shadow of death stain it; let a cloud dwell upon it; let the blackness of the day terrify it.

3:6 As for that night, let darkness seize upon it; let it not be joined unto the days of the year, let it not come into the number of the months. **3:7** Lo, let that night be solitary, let no joyful voice come therein.

3:8 Let them curse it that curse the day, who are ready to raise up their mourning.

3:9 Let the stars of the twilight thereof be dark; let it look for light, but have none; neither let it see the dawning of the day: **3:10** Because it shut not up the doors of my mother's womb, nor hid sorrow from mine eyes.

Job laments in his suffering that it would have been far better to not have even been born.

3:11 Why died I not from the womb? why did I not give up the ghost when I came out of the belly? **3:12** Why did the knees [not hold back from giving birth] prevent me? or why [were] the breasts [full of milk] that I should suck? **3:13** For now should I have lain still and been quiet [in death], I should have slept: then had I been at rest [from all this suffering of body and spirit],

Job wanted to be dead, which is the end of all flesh from the greatest to the least; so that his suffering would also end.

3:14 With kings and counsellors of the earth, which build desolate places [graves] for themselves; **3:15** Or with princes that had gold, who filled their houses with silver: **3:16** Or as an hidden untimely birth [so that] I had not been; as infants which never saw light.

3:17 There the wicked cease from troubling; and there the weary be at rest. **3:18** There the prisoners rest together; they hear not the voice of the oppressor. **3:19** The small and great are there; and the servant is free from his master.

Job asks: Why live only to suffer?

3:20 Wherefore is light given to him that is in misery, and life unto the bitter in soul; **3:21** Which long for death, but it cometh not; and dig [seek death] for it more than for hid treasures; **3:22** Which rejoice exceedingly, and are glad, when they can find the grave? **3:23** Why is light given to a man whose way is hid, and whom God hath hedged in? **3:24** For my sighing cometh before I eat, and my roarings are poured out like the waters.

Job had trusted in his wealth and children fearing to lose them; God was teaching him to put his trust in God and not in physical things..

3:25 For the thing which I greatly feared is come upon me, and that which I was afraid of is come unto me. **3:26** I was not in safety [he feared], neither had I rest [relaxed and free of fear], neither was I quiet [Job did not have peace of mind]; yet trouble [the thing he feared, loss of wealth and family came upon him] came.

Job 4

Eliphaz the Temanite tries to answer Job.

Job 4:1 Then Eliphaz the Temanite answered and said, **4:2** If we assay to commune with thee, wilt thou be grieved? [will you listen to us?] but who can withhold himself from speaking?

You have taught and helped many and now that you have your own trials you forget your own councils and faint away.

4:3 Behold, thou hast instructed many, and thou hast strengthened the weak hands. **4:4** Thy words have upholden him that was falling, and thou hast strengthened the feeble knees. **4:5** But now it [this trial] is come upon thee, and thou faintest; it toucheth thee, and thou art troubled.

With that truthful opening, Eliphaz then begins to reason that since the wicked will be ultimately cut off; that means that ALL suffering [and sickness] is because of some wickedness.

Jesus Christ gave the answer to these questions.

> **John 9:1** And as Jesus passed by, he saw a man which was blind from his birth.

9:2 And his disciples asked him, saying, Master, who did sin, this man, or his parents, that he was born blind?

9:3 Jesus answered, **Neither hath this man sinned, nor his parents: but that the works of God should be made manifest in him.**

Eliphaz argues that Job must have sinned and that the God who judges angels is judging Job for his sin.

Job 4:6 Is not this thy fear, thy confidence, thy hope, and the uprightness of thy ways? **4:7** Remember, I pray thee, who ever perished, being innocent? or where were the righteous cut off? **4:8** Even as I have seen, they that plow iniquity, and sow wickedness, reap the same.

4:9 By the blast of God they perish, and by the breath of his nostrils are they consumed. **4:10** The roaring of the lion [mighty man , and the voice of the fierce lion [powerful man] , and the teeth of the young lions [strong young men], are broken. **4:11** The old lion perisheth for lack of prey, and the stout lion's whelps are scattered abroad.

The greatness of God

4:12 Now a thing was secretly brought to me, and mine ear received a little thereof. **4:13** In thoughts from the visions of the night, when deep sleep falleth on men, **4:14** Fear came upon me, and trembling, which made all my bones to shake.

4:15 Then a spirit passed before my face; the hair of my flesh stood up: **4:16** It stood still, but I could not discern the form thereof: an image was before mine eyes, there was silence, and I heard a voice, saying,

4:17 Shall mortal man be more just than God? shall a man be more pure than his maker? 4:18 Behold, he put no trust in his servants; and his [fallen] angels he charged with folly: **4:19** How much less in them that dwell in houses of clay [God will not be concerned with fleshly men] , whose foundation is in the dust, which are crushed before the moth? **4:20** They are destroyed from morning to evening: they perish for ever without any regarding it. **4:21** Doth not their excellency which is in them go away? they die, even without wisdom.

Job 5

Job 5:1 Call now, if there be any that will answer [no one can defend against God] thee; and to which of the saints wilt thou turn? **5:2** For wrath killeth the foolish man, and envy slayeth the silly one.

5:3 I have seen the foolish taking root [prospering]: but suddenly I [God] cursed his habitation. **5:4** His [the wicked man's] children are far from safety, and they are crushed in the gate, neither is there any to deliver them. **5:5** Whose [the wicked man's] harvest the hungry eateth up, and taketh [the wealth of the wicked is removed completely from him] it even out of the thorns, and the robber swalloweth up their substance.

He argues that man's afflictions do not come from nothing, but from his own folly and sin.

5:6 Although affliction cometh not forth of the dust, neither doth trouble spring out of the ground; **5:7** Yet man is born unto trouble, as the sparks fly upward.

Eliphas advises Job to repent of his sin and seek out God who has wrought his correction.

5:8 I would seek unto God, and unto God would I commit my cause: **5:9** Which doeth great things and unsearchable; marvellous things without number: **5:10** Who giveth rain upon the earth, and sendeth waters upon the fields: **5:11** To set up on high those that be low; that those which mourn may be exalted to safety.

Job is told not to be crafty or to think that he can outwit God and hide his sins

5:12 He [God] disappointeth the devices of the crafty, so that their hands cannot perform their enterprise. **5:13** He taketh the [worldly] wise in their own craftiness: and the counsel of the froward [stubborn, herd hearted] is carried headlong [to destruction]. **5:14** They meet with darkness in the day time, and grope in the noonday as in the night.

Iniquity is stopped by the humility before God of those who do not trust in physical riches.

5:15 But he saveth the poor from the sword, from their [hunger] mouth, and from the hand of the mighty. **5:16** So the poor [humble in spirit] hath hope, and iniquity stoppeth her mouth.

Happy is the man who responds positively to God's correction, for God will forgive and restore the sincerely repentant.

The blessings of Godliness.

Here Eliphaz misses the point that such blessing are given and taken by God according to God's own will and purposes and not necessarily according to a person's righteousness.

In this world the godly often experience many trials as God molds us into the people he wants us to be for eternity. Yet if we remain faithful to God and zealous to live by every Word of God in blessings and trials; we shall inherit an eternal life.

5:17 Behold, happy is the man whom God correcteth: therefore despise not thou the chastening of the Almighty: **5:18** For he maketh sore, and bindeth up: he woundeth, and his hands make whole.

5:19 He shall deliver thee in six troubles: yea, in seven there shall no evil touch thee. **5:20** In famine he shall redeem thee from death: and in war from the power of the sword. **5:21** Thou shalt be hid from the scourge of the tongue [the faithful shall not fear rebuke] : neither shalt thou be afraid of destruction when it cometh.

5:22 At destruction and famine thou shalt laugh: neither shalt thou be afraid of the beasts of the earth. **5:23** For thou shalt be in league with the stones of the field: and the beasts of the field shall be at peace with thee.

5:24 And thou shalt know that thy tabernacle shall be in peace; and thou shalt visit thy habitation, and shalt not sin.

5:25 Thou shalt know also that thy seed shall be great, and thine offspring as the grass of the earth.

5:26 Thou shalt come to thy grave in a full age, like as a shock of corn cometh in in his season.

5:27 Lo this, we have searched it, so it is; hear it, and know thou it for thy good.

Job 6

Job Answers Eliphaz

Job speaks of his grief and complains that his friend adds to his sorrows instead of consoling him

Job 6:1 But Job answered and said, **6:2** Oh that my grief were throughly weighed, and my calamity laid in the balances together! **6:3** For now it would be heavier than the sand of the sea: therefore my words are swallowed up. **6:4** For the arrows of the Almighty are within me, the poison whereof drinketh up my spirit: the terrors of God do set themselves in array against me.

Would I complain if things were right? Asks Job.

6:5 Doth the wild ass bray when he hath grass? or loweth the ox over his fodder? **6:6** Can that which is unsavoury be eaten without salt? or is there any taste in the white of an egg?

I cannot eat for my sorrows, and must fast.

6:7 The things that my soul refused to touch are as my sorrowful meat.

Here Job makes a mistake common even today! Many people when very ill, have said "let me die". That is a misguided statement, since we really do NOT want to die.

What we really want is relief from our trials and suffering! We say that life in such suffering is not worth living, but what we really want; is healing! We want deliverance from sorrows into a good life well worth living!

6:8 Oh that I might have my request; and that God would grant me the thing that I long for! **6:9 Even that it would please God to destroy me; that he would let loose his hand, and cut me off! 6:10** Then should I yet have comfort; yea, I would harden myself in sorrow: let him not spare; for I have not concealed the words of the Holy One.

Christ had not yet come to reveal a good understanding of human salvation and Christ's sacrifice for the sins of men. Therefore Job argues from the disadvantage of not knowing these spiritual things which were hidden by God until Christ came in the flesh.

Job asks "What is the hope of man except to die and end his sufferings."

6:11 What is my strength, that I should hope? and what is mine end, that I should prolong my life? **6:12** Is my strength the strength of stones? or is my flesh of brass? **6:13** Is not my help in me? and is wisdom driven quite from me?

Job seeks pity from his friends.

6:14 To him that is afflicted pity should be shewed from his friend; but he forsaketh the fear of the Almighty.

Job claims his friends are deceitful in challenging his righteousness and that their accusations will melt away like the snow.

6:15 My brethren have dealt deceitfully as a brook, and as the stream of brooks they pass away; **6:16** Which are blackish by reason of the ice, and wherein the snow is hid: **6:17** What time they wax warm, they vanish: when it is hot, they are consumed out of their place. **6:18** The paths of their way are turned aside; they go to nothing, and perish.

Job claims that his friends are like armies who came to take the spoil and were disappointed that nothing was there.

6:19 The troops of Tema looked, the companies of Sheba waited for them. **6:20** They were confounded because they had hoped; they came thither, and were ashamed.

Job says that in his plenty, his friends took advantage of his generosity; and now that he is afflicted they are upset over the loss of the gifts that Job had given them in the past and are afraid that they will be asked to support Job.

6:21 For now ye are nothing [no help]; ye see my casting down, and are afraid [that Job will ask gifts and alms from them].

Job declares that he wants nothing from them except the truth, so that he may repent of any error.

6:22 Did I say, Bring unto me? or, Give a reward for me of your substance? **6:23** Or, Deliver me from the enemy's hand? or, Redeem me from the hand of the mighty? **6:24 Teach me, and I will hold my tongue: and cause me to understand wherein I have erred.**

Yet, Job declares that the words of his friend are not true and are adding to his affliction by false accusations.

6:25 How forcible [powerful] are right words! but what doth your [false] arguing reprove? **6:26** Do ye imagine to reprove [my] words, and the [with the] speeches of one that is desperate, which are as wind?

Job says: yes, you destroy with false words and dig a grave for me.

6:27 Yea, ye overwhelm the fatherless, and ye dig a pit for your friend.

Look at me and tell me if I lie.

6:28 Now therefore be content, look upon me; for it is evident unto you if I lie.

Job complains that he is made to suffer months without a good reward.

6:29 Return, I pray you, let it not be iniquity; yea, return again, my righteousness is in it. **6:30** Is there iniquity in my tongue [I speak the truth]? cannot my taste discern [what is right and wrong] perverse things?

Job 7

Job 7:1 Is there not an appointed time to man upon earth? are not his days also like the days of an hireling? **7:2** As a servant earnestly desireth the [to rest in the shade] shadow, and as an hireling looketh for the reward of his work: **7:3** So am I made to possess months of vanity, and wearisome nights are appointed to me.

7:4 When I lie down, I say, When shall I arise, and the night be gone? and I am full of tossings to and fro unto the dawning of the day.

7:5 My flesh is clothed with worms [maggots eating the dead flesh of his sores] and clods of dust; my skin is broken, and become loathsome. **7:6** My days are swifter than a weaver's shuttle, and are spent without hope.

Job, without understanding the hope of salvation, sees that his days are passed in suffering and his life has no purpose and will end as all other lives, ending forever in the grave.

This is about the vanity of physical life without God as is the book of Ecclesiastes.

7:7 O remember that my life is wind: mine eye shall no more see good. **7:8** The eye of him that hath seen me shall see me no more: thine eyes are upon me, and I am not. **7:9** As the cloud is consumed and vanisheth away: so he that goeth down to the grave shall come up no more.

Job will not hold his peace since he believes that he has no hope beyond the grave.

7:10 He shall return no more to his house, neither shall his place know him any more. **7:11** Therefore I will not refrain my mouth; I will speak in the anguish of my spirit; I will complain in the bitterness of my soul.

There is no escape from suffering, for when Job is comforted in sleep he is terrorized by dreams.

7:12 Am I a sea, or a whale, that thou settest a watch over me? **7:13** When I say, My bed shall comfort me, my couch shall ease my complaints; **7:14** Then thou scarest me with dreams, and terrifiest me through visions: **7:15** So that my soul chooseth strangling, and death rather than my life.

Job loathes his life of suffering not realizing that God is perfecting him through his suffering.

7:16 I loathe it; I would not live alway: let me alone; for my days are vanity.

Why is God testing and trying man every moment?

7:17 What is man, that thou shouldest magnify him? and that thou shouldest set thine heart upon him? **7:18** And that thou shouldest visit him every morning, and try him every moment?

Job admits that he must have sinned, and asks God's pardon and the lifting of his sorrows before he finds death.

7:19 How long wilt thou not depart from me, nor let me alone [make me to suffer] **till I swallow down my spittle? 7:20 I have sinned;** what shall I do unto thee, O thou preserver of men? why hast thou set me as a mark against thee, so that I am a burden to myself? **7:21** And **why dost thou not pardon my transgression, and take away my iniquity? for now shall I sleep in the dust; and thou shalt seek me in the morning, but I shall not be.**

The answers to all these questions of why God allows suffering and allows even the righteous to suffer, are found in the spiritual teachings of Christ and the apostles.

Correction and trials are for our GOOD, so that we may turn to the Eternal God and be saved. It is often by affliction of the flesh that the spirit can be saved. Therefore do not despise the correction of the LORD who is working to save us like he saved Job.

Do not lose heart and give up; because our trials are only for a very short time compared to eternity and they are tools that Almighty God the Master Potter uses perfect us.

> **Hebrews 12:5** And ye have forgotten the exhortation **which speaketh unto you as unto children, My son, despise not thou the chastening of the Lord, nor faint when thou art rebuked of him: 12:6 For whom the Lord loveth he chasteneth, and scourgeth every son whom he receiveth. 12:7 If ye endure chastening, God dealeth with you as with sons; for what son is he whom the father chasteneth not? 12:8 But if ye be without** [If we refuse to be corrected to learn to obey God our Father, we are not the sons of God] **chastisement, whereof all are partakers, then are ye bastards, and not sons.**

We are not legitimate sons if we will not accept the guidance, instruction and correction of God our Father. To be legitimate sons of God the Father, we must accept and keep every Word of God our Father, and act with repentance upon his correction.

> **12:9** Furthermore **we have had fathers of our flesh which corrected us, and we gave them reverence: shall we not much rather be in subjection unto the Father of spirits, and live** [receive eternal life]? **12:10** For they verily for a few days chastened us after their own pleasure; but he, [God or Christ, corrects us for our advantage, not for his own pleasure.] **for our profit that we might be partakers of his holiness.**

Of course our correction will be grievous and in the flesh we often suffer greatly, but it will bring us to God and his holiness and his gift of eternal life

> **12:11** Now no chastening for the present seemeth to be joyous, but grievous: **nevertheless afterward it yieldeth the peaceable fruit of righteousness** unto them which are exercised thereby

Job 8

Bildad Speaks and Job Answers

Job is humble before God, for God himself declared Job to be perfect in Job 1. The book of Job is about the age old question of why God allows the righteous to suffer in this life. Job is accompanied by Ecclesiastes in the inquiry into this questions of "Is this physical life all there is?" and "Why does God allow the innocent to suffer?".

Job 8:1 Then answered Bildad the Shuhite, and said, [to Job] **8:2** How long wilt thou speak these things? and how long shall the words of thy mouth be like a strong wind? [nothing but air]

He assumes that evil falls only on the evil doer.

8:3 Doth God pervert judgment? or doth the Almighty pervert justice? **8:4** If thy children have sinned against him, and he have cast them away for their transgression; **8:5** If thou wouldest seek unto God betimes, and make thy supplication to the Almighty; **8:6** If thou wert pure and upright; surely now he would awake for thee, and make the habitation of thy righteousness prosperous.

8:7 Though thy beginning was small, yet thy latter end should greatly increase.

Consider history and learn from the wisdom of our forefathers.

8:8 For enquire, I pray thee, of the former age, and prepare thyself to the search of their fathers: **8:9** (For we are but of yesterday, and know nothing, because our days upon earth are a shadow:) **8:10** Shall not they teach thee, and tell thee, and utter words out of their heart? **8:11** Can the rush grow up without mire? can the flag [rushes] grow without water? **8:12** Whilst it is yet in his greenness, and not cut down, it withereth before any other herb.

Learn from our trials to faithfully, patiently, live by every Word of God regardless of trials, for our trials are intended to teach and perfect us.

8:13 So are the paths of all that forget God; and the hypocrite's hope shall perish: **8:14** Whose hope shall be cut off, and whose trust shall be a spider's web.

The commandment breaker will flourish for a short time only to be brought down.

8:15 He shall lean upon [build up] his house, but it shall not stand: he shall hold it fast, but it shall not endure.

The wicked is as a green shoot that has no root and withers in the sun.

8:16 He is green before the sun, and his branch shooteth forth in his garden. **8:17** His roots are wrapped about the heap, and seeth the place of stones.

It is the will of God that the wicked who tolerate sin be rooted up.

8:18 If he destroy him from his place, then it shall deny him, saying, I have not seen thee. **8:19** Behold, this is the joy of his [God's] way, and out of the earth shall others [more faithful] grow.

The error of Bildad lies in not acknowledging that God does as he pleases to mold men and purge them so that they become what God wants for them. Bildad is denying the sovereignty of God to do his own will.

Jesus Christ came to reveal that God purges the righteous so that they will bring forth more good fruit (John 15).

8:20 Behold, God will not cast away a perfect man, neither will he help the evil doers: **8:21** Till he fill thy mouth with laughing, and thy lips with rejoicing.

8:22 They that hate thee [those that hate God's law and his commandment keepers] shall be clothed with shame; and the dwelling place of the wicked shall come to nought.

Job 9

Job says that he knows that God will lift up the righteous and destroy the wicked, but asks how can any man be justified before God?

Jesus taught that the reward for those who live by every Word of God will be at the resurrection, not necessarily in this life. The wicked will persecute the righteous, and God will allow that to happen to mold the righteous through experience; as he himself learned through his own suffering (Heb 5:8).

Jesus Christ also came to reveal the way to salvation and to lay down his life for the repentant.

Job 9:1 Then Job answered and said, **9:2** I know it is so of a truth: but how should man be just with [before] God? **9:3** If he will contend with him, he cannot answer him one of a thousand.

Job then speaks of the greatness of God in true humility before God.

No proud self-righteous person could speak of God in the following words and declare that man cannot justify themselves before God!

Job, is genuinely humble before God, and most religious folks have committed the same sin as Job's three friends in accusing Job of sin.

Indeed Job had just asked God to forgive any sin that he had done in **Job 7: 20 I have sinned;** what shall I do unto thee, O thou preserver of men? why hast thou set me as a mark against thee, so that I am a burden to myself? **7:21** And why dost thou not pardon my transgression, and take away my iniquity? for now shall I sleep in the dust; and thou shalt seek me in the morning, but I shall not be.

Job's humility before the greatness of God

Job 9:4 He [God] is wise in heart, and mighty in strength: who hath [can] hardened himself against him [God], and hath prospered? **9:5** Which removeth the mountains, and they know not: which overturneth them in his anger. **9:6** Which shaketh the earth out of her place, and the pillars thereof tremble.

9:7 Which commandeth the sun, and it riseth not; and sealeth up the stars. **9:8** Which alone spreadeth out the heavens, and treadeth upon the waves of the sea. **9:9** Which maketh Arcturus, Orion, and Pleiades, and the chambers of the south. **9:10** Which doeth great things past finding out; yea, and wonders without number.

9:11 Lo, he goeth by me, and I see him not: he passeth on also, but I perceive him not. **9:12** Behold, he taketh away, who can hinder him? who will say unto him, What doest thou? **9:13** If God will not withdraw his anger, the proud helpers do stoop under him.

Job is so humble and fearful of God that he does not dare dispute with God, Job would only make supplication to God and not dispute with God.

9:14 How much less shall I answer him, and choose out my words to reason with him? **9:15** Whom, though [even if] I were righteous, yet would I not answer, but I would make supplication to my judge.

Job knows that God has allowed him to be battered, yet he would not dispute with God or sin with his lips (Job 2:10), against God. He would only make supplication in repentance for anything he might have done wrong.

Job knows the power of God because he has suffered and he cannot understand why, yet he remains faithful to God.

9:16 If I had called, and he had answered me; yet would I not believe that he had hearkened unto my voice. **9:17** For he breaketh me with a tempest, and multiplieth my wounds without cause. **9:18** He will not suffer me to take my breath, but filleth me with bitterness.

Job speaks the truth that men cannot justify themselves before God.

9:19 If I speak of strength, lo, he is strong: and if of judgment, who shall set me a time to plead? **9:20** If I justify myself, mine own mouth shall condemn me: if I say, I am perfect, it shall also prove me perverse.

9:21 Though [if] I were perfect, yet would I [I would still not see every hidden sin] not know my soul: I would [still be nothing before God] despise my life.

Job admits that God has power over all things, both the wicked and the innocent.

9:22 This is one thing, therefore I said it, He destroyeth the perfect and the wicked. **9:23** If the scourge slay suddenly, he will laugh at the trial of the innocent.

God allows wickedness on the earth to teach us to abhor all sin.

9:24 The earth is given into the hand of the wicked: he covereth the faces of the judges thereof; if not, where, and who is he?

The lifespan of man is as the wind; this is vanity; for physical life has no purpose if it ends with the grave.

9:25 Now my days are swifter than a post: they flee away, they see no good. **9:26** They are passed away as the swift ships: as the eagle that hasteth to the prey.

If we try to find comfort and do not seek out the meaning of our sorrows we would learn nothing and would not be guiltless before God. In this Job begins to acknowledge that God is trying to teach him something with this trial.

9:27 If I say, I will forget my complaint, I will leave off my heaviness, and comfort myself: **9:28** I am afraid of all my sorrows, I know that thou wilt not hold me innocent.

9:29 If I be wicked, why then labour [to be righteous] I in vain? **9:30** If I wash myself with snow water, and make my hands never so clean; **9:31** Yet shalt thou plunge me in the ditch, and mine own clothes shall abhor me.

Job will not equate himself with God as today's Ekklesia does. Job is humble before God, but these groups equate loyalty to themselves with loyalty to God.

9:32 For he is not a man, as I am, that I should answer him, and we should come together in judgment.

There was no intercessor between man and God until Jesus Christ was accepted to that role on Wave Offering Sunday.

9:33 Neither is there any daysman [intercessor Strong's 3198] betwixt us, that might lay his hand upon us both.

Job asks for mercy, he asks why this thing has come upon him

9:34 Let him take his rod away from me, and let not his fear terrify me:
9:35 Then would I speak, and not fear him; but it is not so with me.

Job 10

Job 10:1 My soul is weary of my life; I will leave my complaint upon myself; I will speak in the bitterness of my soul. **10:2** I will say unto God, Do not condemn me; **shew me wherefore thou contendest with me.**

Job asks if God can have compassion on man, not having experienced what it is to be flesh. It was for this reason among many others that the Creator was made flesh,

> **Hebrews 2:17** Wherefore in all things it behoved him to be made like unto his brethren, that he might be a merciful and faithful high priest in things pertaining to God, to make reconciliation for the sins of the people. **2:18** For in that he himself hath suffered being tempted, he is able to succour them that are tempted.

Job 10:3 Is it good unto thee that thou shouldest oppress, that thou shouldest despise the work of thine hands, and shine upon the counsel of the wicked? **10:4** Hast thou eyes of flesh? or seest thou as man seeth? **10:5** Are thy days as the days of man? are thy years as man's days, **10:6** That thou enquirest after mine iniquity, and searchest after my sin? **10:7** Thou knowest that I am not wicked; and there is none that can deliver out of thine hand.

10:8 Thine hands have made me and fashioned me together round about; yet thou dost destroy me. **10:9** Remember, I beseech thee, that thou hast made me as the clay; and wilt thou bring me into dust again? **10:10** Hast thou not poured me out as milk, and curdled me like cheese? **10:11** Thou hast clothed me with skin and flesh, and hast fenced me with bones and sinews.

10:12 Thou hast granted me life and favour, and thy visitation hath preserved my spirit. **10:13** And these things hast thou hid in thine heart: I know that this is with thee. **10:14** If I sin, then thou markest me, and thou wilt not acquit me from mine iniquity.

Job is confused that both the wicked and the righteous are afflicted and the end of both is death.

10:15 If I be wicked, woe unto me; and if I be righteous, yet will I not lift up my head. **I am full of confusion**; therefore see thou mine affliction; **10:16** For it increaseth. Thou huntest me as a fierce lion: and again thou shewest thyself marvellous upon me.

One lesson of Job is that there is none righteous in comparison to God. Even the most righteous man has at some time sinned and needs to be reconciled to God. If there is nothing beyond the grave, what value is there in this physical life?

10:17 Thou renewest thy witnesses against me, and increasest thine indignation upon me; changes and war are against me.

10:18 Wherefore then hast thou brought me forth out of the womb? Oh that I had given up the ghost, and no eye had seen me! **10:19** I should have been as though I had not been; I should have been carried from the womb to the grave.

10:20 Are not my days few? cease then, and let me alone, that I may take comfort a little, **10:21 Before I go whence I shall not return, even to the land of darkness and the shadow of death; 10:22 A land of darkness, as darkness itself; and of the shadow of death, without any order, and where the light is as darkness.**

Job 11

Zophar Speaks and Job Answers

The suffering of Job is an example of Job's steadfast loyalty in the face of extreme suffering; an example for us to follow in being diligently faithful in living by every Word of God throughout all our trials and in the good times as well.

Zophar asks if a man is justified by multitudes of words. He attacks Job for saying that he is clean from sin.

Job 11:1 Then answered Zophar the Naamathite, and said, **11:2** Should not the multitude of words be answered? and should a man full of talk be justified? **11:3** Should thy lies make men hold their peace? and when thou mockest, shall no man make thee ashamed? **11:4** For thou hast said, My doctrine is pure, and I am clean in thine eyes.

Job is condemned by his friend

11:5 But oh that God would speak, and open his lips against thee; **11:6** And that he would shew thee the secrets of wisdom, that they are double to that which is! Know therefore that God exacteth of thee less than thine iniquity deserveth.

The greatness of God

11:7 Canst thou by searching find out God? canst thou find out the Almighty unto perfection? **11:8** It is as high as heaven; what canst thou do? deeper than hell; what canst thou know? **11:9** The measure thereof is longer than the earth, and broader than the sea. **11:10** If he cut off, and shut up, or gather together, then who can hinder him? **11:11** For he knoweth vain men: he seeth wickedness also; will he not then consider it? **11:12** For vain men would be wise, though man be born like a wild ass's colt.

Job is urged to repent and Zophar speaks the truth about repentance

11:13 If thou prepare thine heart, and stretch out thine hands toward him; **11:14** If iniquity be in thine hand, put it far away, and let not wickedness dwell in thy tabernacles. **11:15** For then shalt thou lift up thy face without spot; yea, thou shalt be stedfast, and shalt not fear: **11:16** Because thou shalt forget thy misery, and remember it as waters that pass away: **11:17** And thine age shall be clearer than the noonday: thou shalt shine forth, thou shalt be as the morning.

11:18 And thou shalt be secure, because there is hope; yea, thou shalt dig about thee, and thou shalt take thy rest in safety. **11:19** Also thou shalt lie down, and none shall make thee afraid; yea, many shall make suit unto thee.

Zophar speaks the truth about the wicked; still failing to understand that God uses trials to build character and to test those he is calling.

11:20 But the eyes of the wicked shall fail, and they shall not escape, and their hope shall be as the giving up of the ghost.

Job 12

Job Answers

Job 12:1 And Job answered and said, **12:2** No doubt but ye are the people, and wisdom shall die with you.

Job complains that the just [godly] are laughed at when they have trials.

12:3 But I have understanding as well as you; I am not inferior to you: yea, who knoweth not [does not know this] such things as these? **12:4** I am as one mocked of his neighbour, who calleth upon God, and he answereth him: the just upright man is laughed to scorn. **12:5** He that is ready to slip with his feet [those is trouble] is as a lamp despised in the thought of him that is at ease.

Job begins to see that the wicked often prosper and the faithful often suffer.

12:6 The tabernacles of robbers prosper, and they that provoke God are secure; into whose hand God bringeth abundantly.

12:7 But ask now the beasts, and they shall teach thee; and the fowls of the air, and they shall tell thee: **12:8** Or speak to the earth, and it shall teach thee: and the fishes of the sea shall declare unto thee. **12:9** Who knoweth not in all these that the hand of the LORD hath wrought this? **12:10** In whose hand is the soul of every living thing, and the breath of all mankind.

God is the most ancient and wisest of all. Job says that God knows his sins or righteousness.

12:11 Doth not the ear try words? and the mouth taste his meat? **12:12** With the ancient is wisdom; and in length of days understanding. **12:13** With him [God] is wisdom and strength, he hath counsel and understanding. **12:14** Behold, he breaketh down, and it cannot be built again: he shutteth up a man, and there can be no opening.

12:15 Behold, he withholdeth the waters, and they dry up: also he sendeth them out, and they overturn the earth. **12:16** With him is strength and wisdom: the deceived and the deceiver are his.

12:17 He leadeth counsellors away spoiled, and maketh the judges fools. **12:18** He looseth the bond of kings, and girdeth their loins with a girdle. **12:19** He leadeth princes away spoiled, and overthroweth the mighty. **12:20** He removeth away the speech of the trusty, and taketh away the understanding of the aged.

12:21 He poureth contempt upon princes, and weakeneth the strength of the mighty. **12:22** He discovereth deep things out of darkness, and bringeth out to light the shadow of death. **12:23** He increaseth the nations, and destroyeth them: he enlargeth the nations, and straiteneth them again.

12:24 He taketh away the heart of the chief of the people of the earth, and causeth them to wander in a wilderness where there is no way. **12:25** They grope in the dark without light, and he maketh them to stagger like a drunken man.

Job 13

Job 13:1 Lo, mine eye hath seen all this, mine ear hath heard and understood it.

Job complains that he knows the things his friends are saying about sin and about God are true, but that he knows that he is innocent of sin in the eyes of God.

13:2 What ye know, the same do I know also: I am not inferior unto you. **13:3** Surely I would speak to the Almighty, and I desire to reason with God.

Job responds to being by saying that his friends have become false accusers, who are not helping him.

13:4 But ye are forgers of lies, ye are all physicians of no value. **13:5** O that ye would altogether hold your peace! and it should be your wisdom.

Job presents his case

13:6 Hear now my reasoning, and hearken to the pleadings of my lips.

Job says: Do not mock God by calling him unrighteous for my affliction if I have not sinned. Job knows that he has not sinned yet Job will not allow his sufferings to cause him to speak against God; Job is faithful in good times and in sorrows.

13:7 Will ye speak wickedly for God? and talk deceitfully for him? **13:8** Will ye accept his person? will ye contend for God? **13:9** Is it good that he should search you out? or as one man mocketh another, do ye so mock him? **13:10** He will surely reprove you, if ye do secretly accept persons.

13:11 Shall not his excellency make you afraid? and his dread fall upon you? **13:12** Your remembrances are like unto ashes, your bodies to bodies of clay. **13:13** Hold your peace, let me alone, that I may speak, and let come on me what will.

Job places his trust in God's hands in spite of his sorrows.

13:14 Wherefore do I take my flesh in my teeth, and put my life in mine hand? **13:15 Though he slay me, yet will I trust in him: but I will maintain mine own** [godly obedience] **ways before him. 13:16 He also shall be my salvation:** for an hypocrite shall not come before him.

Job is faithful to God and Job knows that God will ultimately justify God's faithful

13:17 Hear diligently my speech, and my declaration with your ears. **13:18** Behold now, I have ordered my cause; I know that I shall be justified.

13:19 Who is he that will plead [argue] with me? for now, if I hold my tongue, I shall give up the ghost. **13:20** Only do not two things unto me: then will I not hide myself from thee.

Job pleads with God, asking God not to withdraw from Job and asking God to always keep Job in fear [worshipful respect] of God.

13:21 Withdraw thine hand far from me: and let not thy dread make me afraid.

Job asks God to reveal to Job any sin that he has committed

13:22 Then call thou, and I will answer: or let me speak, and answer thou me. **13:23** How many are mine iniquities and sins? make me to know my transgression and my sin.

Job asks why God has hidden himself from Job and given Job over to the Adversary.

13:24 Wherefore hidest thou thy face, and holdest me for thine enemy? **13:25** Wilt thou break a leaf driven to and fro? and wilt thou pursue the dry stubble? **13:26** For thou writest bitter things against me, and makest me to possess the iniquities of my youth.

13:27 Thou puttest my feet also in the stocks, and lookest narrowly unto all my paths; thou settest a print upon the heels of my feet. **13:28** And he [the Adversary], as a rotten thing, consumeth, as a garment that is moth eaten.

Job 14

Job says that he and all flesh are unclean before God

Job 14:1 Man that is born of a woman is of few days and full of trouble. **14:2** He cometh forth like a flower, and is cut down: he fleeth also as a shadow, and continueth not.

14:3 And doth thou open thine eyes upon such an one, and bringest me into judgment with thee? **14:4** Who can bring a clean thing out of an unclean? not one.

Job asks for compassion and a life of rest until he dies. for he does not know of any resurrection and believes that this physical life is all there is. This speaks of the vanity of physical life and the need for God's deliverance from death, as does Ecclesiastes.

14:5 Seeing his days are determined, the number of his months are with thee, thou hast appointed his bounds that he cannot pass; **14:6** Turn from him, that he may rest, till he shall accomplish, as an hireling, his day.

14:7 For there is hope of a tree, if it be cut down, that it will sprout again, and that the tender branch thereof will not cease. **14:8** Though the root thereof wax old in the earth, and the stock thereof die in the ground; **14:9** Yet through the scent of water it will bud, and bring forth boughs like a plant.

14:10 But man dieth, and wasteth away: yea, man giveth up the ghost, and where is he? **14:11** As the waters fail from the sea, and the flood decayeth and drieth up: **14:12** So man lieth down, and riseth not: till the heavens be no more, they shall not awake, nor be raised out of their sleep.

Job now longs for a resurrection from the grave; perhaps for the first time putting the concept of a resurrection in the scriptures!

14:13 O that thou wouldest hide me in the grave, that thou wouldest keep me secret, **until thy wrath be past, that thou wouldest appoint me a set time, and remember me! 14:14** If a man die, shall he live again? all the days of my appointed time will I wait, till my change come. **14:15** Thou shalt call, and I will answer thee: thou wilt have a desire to the work of thine hands.

Oh, that our sins would be sewed up in a sack and destroyed from us! For the first time in scripture; spiritual salvation is spoken of and longed for! Job longs for something more than a physical life followed by the grave! He asks why sin cannot be removed and why there is no hope for man.

This is profound as it opens the way for Messiah and salvation.

14:16 For now thou numberest my steps: dost thou not watch over my sin? **14:17** My transgression is sealed up in a bag, and thou sewest up mine iniquity.

14:18 And surely the mountains falling cometh to nought, and the rock is removed out of his place. **14:19** The waters wear the stones: thou washest away the things which grow out of the dust of the earth; and thou destroyest the hope of man.

14:20 Thou prevailest for ever against him, and he passeth: thou changest his countenance, and sendest him away. **14:21** His sons come to honour, and he knoweth it not; and they are brought low, but he perceiveth it not of them. **14:22** But his flesh upon him shall have pain, and his soul within him shall mourn.

I once heard a speaker characterize the book of Job as tedious and confusing, saying it will only confuse people; actually discouraging people from reading the book. The speaker then took one sentence from Chap 40 totally out of context to wrongly claim that one line is what the whole book was about. I am sure he did not realize that he was attacking God's Word, for all scripture is inspired by God and is for our instruction.

Job is full of inspired wisdom from both Job and his friends. Although his friends make the error of wrongly blaming Job for sin, and for saying that if God was afflicting Job and that if Job had no sin, that God was unrighteous; therefore concluding that Job was sinful: They were absolutely right in saying that sin brings destruction and obedience to God brings life, just not understanding that physical life was a growing overcoming process to build the character that will endure for eternity.

This is a very "deep" book filled with truths. The way to study Job is to do it section by section with the statements and responses. How anyone could say that this book is tedious with its profound truths and majestic descriptions of God and his ways is baffling to me.

This man also said that even the scholars were confused! That is because they are not converted and cannot understand spiritual things.

I do not fault this speaker overmuch, he is just teaching what he has been taught; but it is long past time that we opened our eyes to the majesty of ALL of God's Word.

The Second Eliphaz Discourse

Job is about loyalty to God in the face of severe trials; and the question of why the righteous suffer.

God tests his people, and through that testing we are made stronger if we persevere! Who has not heard of the sacrifice of Isaac, the promised son of Abraham's old age? or Joseph's years in prison; or the trials of all the faithful saints (Heb 11)?

Every person who is truly called out, from every generation; has his faith and loyalty tested!

God's people have been and are being tested, just like our forefathers: and the test is about patient persevering loyalty to God!

Will we be loyal to God and live by God's Word? or will we be more loyal to human organizations, the traditions of men and religious executives?

Do we equate loyalty to some man, tradition or organization; with loyalty to God? Which IS IDOLATRY! Or are we zealous and faithfully loyal to our espoused Husband and Mighty God in all circumstances; whether in blessings or in severe trials?

Job 15

Job is accused of foolishness

Job 15:1 Then answered Eliphaz the Temanite, and said, **15:2** Should a wise man utter vain knowledge, and fill his belly with the east wind? **15:3** Should he reason with unprofitable talk? or with speeches wherewith he can do no good? **15:4** Yea, thou castest off fear, and restrainest prayer before God. **15:5** For thy mouth uttereth thine iniquity, and thou choosest the tongue of the crafty. **15:6** Thine own mouth condemneth thee, and not I: yea, thine own lips testify against thee.

Eliphaz claims to be much older than Job and that therefore Job should bow to the "wisdom" of his aged friends and not answer them back.

15:7 Art thou the first man that was born? or wast thou made before the hills? **15:8** Hast thou heard the secret of God? and dost thou restrain wisdom to thyself? **15:9** What knowest thou, that we know not? what understandest thou, which is not in us? **15:10** With us are both the grayheaded and very aged men, much elder than thy father.

He claims that Job resists God when Job is doing nothing of the kind. Job does not sin against God; he merely asks: WHY Lord?

15:11 Are the consolations of God small with thee? is there any secret thing with thee? **15:12** Why doth thine heart carry thee away? and what do thy eyes wink at, **15:13** That thou turnest thy spirit against God, and lettest such words go out of thy mouth? **15:14** What is man, that he should be clean? and he which is born of a woman, that he should be righteous? **15:15** Behold, he putteth no trust in his saints; yea, the heavens are not clean in his sight.

Eliphaz speaks of the fate of the wicked [which is true] but he declares Job to be wicked because he has trials [which is false].

15:16 How much more abominable and filthy is man, which drinketh iniquity like water? **15:17** I will shew thee, hear me; and that which I have seen I will declare; **15:18** Which wise men have told from their fathers, and have not hid it: **15:19** Unto whom alone the earth was given, and no stranger passed among them.

15:20 The wicked man travaileth with pain all his days, and the number of years is hidden to the oppressor. **15:21** A dreadful sound is in his ears: in prosperity the destroyer shall come upon him. **15:22** He believeth not that he shall return out of darkness, and he is waited for of the sword. **15:23** He wandereth abroad for bread, saying, Where is it? he knoweth that the day of darkness is ready at his hand.

15:24 Trouble and anguish shall make him afraid; they shall prevail against him, as a king ready to the battle. **15:25** For he stretcheth out his hand against God, and strengtheneth himself against the Almighty. **15:26** He [God resists the proud and wicked] runneth upon him, even on his neck, upon the thick bosses of his bucklers: **15:27** Because he covereth his face with his fatness, and maketh collops of fat on his flanks.

15:28 And he [the wicked is brought to desolation] dwelleth in desolate cities, and in houses which no man inhabiteth, which are ready to become heaps. **15:29** He shall not be rich, neither shall his substance continue, neither shall he prolong the perfection thereof upon the earth. **15:30** He shall not depart out of darkness; the flame shall dry up his branches, and by the breath of his mouth shall he go away.

15:31 Let not him that is deceived trust in [the emptiness of wickedness and rebellion against God] vanity: for vanity shall be his recompence. **15:32** It shall be accomplished before his time, and his branch shall not be green. **15:33** He shall shake off his unripe grape as the vine, and shall cast off his flower as the olive.

15:34 For the congregation of hypocrites shall be desolate, and fire shall consume the tabernacles of bribery. **15:35** They [commandment breakers] conceive mischief, and bring forth vanity, and their belly prepareth deceit.

Job 16

Job Answers Eliphaz

The Second Discourse

Job complains that his friends are no comfort and they accuse him wrongfully.

Job 16:1 Then Job answered and said, **16:2** I have heard many such things: miserable comforters are ye all.

Job admits that he would accuse his friends in the same manner if their roles were reversed. This argument is about the knotty question of why God allows sorrows to befall righteous people.

16:3 Shall vain words have an end? or what emboldeneth thee that thou answerest? **16:4** I also could speak as ye do: if your soul were in my soul's stead, I could heap up words against you, and shake mine head at you.

Job says that he would encourage and not just accuse.

16:5 But I would strengthen you with my mouth, and the moving of my lips should asswage your grief.

Whether Job speaks or is silent, he has no comfort, for God has allowed him to be made desolate.

16:6 Though I speak, my grief is not asswaged [eased]: and though I forbear, what am I eased? **16:7** But now he [God] hath made me weary: thou hast made desolate all my company. **16:8** And thou hast filled me with wrinkles, which is a witness against me: and my leanness rising up in me beareth witness to my face.

God has allowed Job's enemies to overcome him.

16:9 He teareth me in his wrath, who hateth me: he gnasheth upon me with his teeth; mine enemy sharpeneth his eyes upon me. **16:10** They have gaped upon me with their mouth; they have smitten me upon the cheek reproachfully; they have gathered themselves together against me.

16:11 God hath delivered me to the ungodly, and turned me over into the hands of the wicked. 16:12 I was at ease, but he hath broken me asunder: he hath also taken me by my neck, and shaken me to pieces, and set me up for his mark. **16:13** His archers compass me round about, he cleaveth my reins asunder, and doth not spare; he poureth out my gall upon the ground.

16:14 He breaketh me with breach upon breach, he runneth upon me like a giant. **16:15** I have sewed sackcloth upon my skin, and defiled my horn [strength] in the dust. **16:16** My face is foul with weeping, and on my eyelids is the shadow of death;

Job is pure and perfect before God, as God himself has said; yet Job does NOT sin against God by accusing God of wrongdoing in allowing his suffering; instead Job seeks mercy and pleads with God for relief.

This is about Satan's attempts to break Job's loyalty to God, and about the question of why God allows the good to suffer!

Job's loyalty to God was being tested ,just like we are tested day by day in many ways; often being asked to equate loyalty to God with loyalty to men, traditions and organizations.

Job passed the test, but we are failing because we exalt men, organizations and the traditions of men above the Word of God, and then we seek to moderate our trials by compromising with the Word of God; a thing that JOB DID NOT DO.

Job was loyal to God throughout all his testing, while many of us are falling away from our loyalty to God during our own testing.

Job is not suffering for any personal sin, he is being tested and perfected by God.

16:17 Not for any injustice in mine hands: also my prayer is pure. **16:18** O earth, cover not thou my blood, and let my cry have no place.

Job asks to be delivered and not die and be permanently buried in the earth, and he asks that his cries for mercy not fall on deaf ears only to be ignored.

God knows us and our loyalty to HIM! Even in our trials!

16:19 Also now, behold, my witness is in heaven, and my record is on high.

The friends of the righteous often scorn those who fall into trials; not understanding that God is testing his people and purging them so that they might bring forth abundant fruit in God's good time.

16:20 My friends scorn me: but mine eye poureth out tears unto God.

Job pleads for deliverance by God, seeking relief.

16:21 O that one might plead for a man with God, as a man pleadeth for his neighbour! **16:22** When a few years are come, then I shall go the way whence I shall not return.

Job says that he is only flesh and will die in a few years and asks to be delivered from his sorrows.

Job 17

Job 17:1 My breath is corrupt, my days are extinct, the graves are ready for me.

Mockers and accusers of the righteous will not be exalted in that day.

17:2 Are there not mockers with me? and doth not mine eye continue in their provocation? **17:3** Lay down now, put me in a surety with thee; who is he that will strike [shake hands in agreement] hands with me? **17:4** For thou hast hid their heart from understanding: therefore shalt thou not exalt them.

Neither shall flatters be accepted before God. God wants those who are loyal to him and obey him in spirit and in TRUTH.

17:5 He that speaketh flattery to his friends, even the eyes of his children shall fail.

God has made Job [and the zealously loyal to every Word of God] an execration n this world; yet in due time God will deliver them and exalt them for their zeal and loyalty to God and their faithfulness to live by every Word of God even in extremely adverse situations.

17:6 He hath made me also [oftentimes the zealously loyal to God are seen as] a byword of the people; and [when] **aforetime** I was as a [beautiful instrument]tabret. **17:7** Mine eye also is dim [full of tears] by reason of sorrow, and all my members are as a shadow.

Through these trials the upright will be made stronger, and zeal will be stirred up against the evil doers.

17:8 Upright men shall be astonied at this, and the innocent shall stir up himself against the hypocrite. **17:9** The righteous also shall hold on his way, and he that hath clean hands shall be stronger and stronger. **17:10** But as for you all, do ye return, and come now: for I cannot find one wise man among you.

Job now laments that his life is over and he faces the grave because of his trials..

Job remains absolutely loyal to God even without the promise of eternal life, honestly believing that there is no reward for his faithfulness and loyalty except the grave which is common with the wicked.

Job is not loyal to God for reward; he is absolutely loyal to God and every Word of God out of love and respect!

17:11 My days are past, my purposes are broken off, even the thoughts of my heart. **17:12** They change the night into day: the light is short because of darkness. **17:13** If I wait, the grave is mine house: I have made my bed in the darkness.

17:14 I have said to corruption, Thou art my father: to the worm [maggot], Thou art my mother, and my sister. **17:15** And where is now my hope? as for my hope, who shall see it? **17:16** They shall go down to the bars of the pit [grave], when our rest together is in the dust.

Bildad's Second Discourse

We are getting into some really solid meat about the meaning of Job; which is much deeper and different from what most teach. Please read this slowly and give it some serious thought.

Bildad asks how long will Job regard his friends as stupid and lacking knowledge? He then assumes that Job is an evildoer and proceeds to list the awful fate of evildoers.

Bildad is absolutely correct in his description of the fate of commandment breakers [brethren take note]; but he is in error in condemning Job just because Job is suffering.

Many religious folks fall into the same error as Job's friends, in proclaiming that all sickness is the result of some sin! They simply did [do not] not understand that the book of Job is about the trials and faithfulness of the righteous.

It is self-righteous to condemn others just because they suffer.

There is a very carnal self-righteous tendency to condemn the stricken, just because they are stricken; and to judge by the hearing of the ears and the seeing of the eyes according to our own carnal thinking; instead of judging the heart and spirit as God judges, for God himself said that Job was perfect in righteousness.

The churches misunderstand the Book of Job almost completely. WHY? Because they have the same self-righteous outlook and attitude as Job's three friends!

It was Job's three friends and many today who were / are self-righteous and wrong; priding ourselves on our numbers, income and wealth as a sign of our righteousness before God, and looking on the afflicted as sinners; misunderstanding that God afflicts [corrects] those he loves, not necessarily because they have sinned, but to bring them into even greater perfection just as Jesus Christ learned through the things that He suffered (Heb 5:8).

> **Job 42:7** And it was so, that after the Lord had spoken these words unto Job, the Lord said to Eliphaz the Temanite, **My wrath is kindled against thee, and against thy two friends: for ye have not spoken of me the thing that is right,** as my servant Job hath.
>
> **42:8** Therefore take unto you now seven bullocks and seven rams, and **go to my servant Job, and offer up for yourselves a burnt offering; and my servant Job shall pray for you: for him will I accept: lest I deal with you after your folly, in that ye have not spoken of me the thing which is right**, like my servant Job.

Brethren, today the major Groups in the Spiritual Ekklesia are apostate from any zeal for the practical application of God's Word. They are proud and self-righteous, doing as they think right instead of enthusiastically obeying God. They justify themselves and they attack the messenger who warns them in love, seeking to save them.

I will cover this more thoroughly when I get to Job 42; where Job, who did not understand why he had been afflicted, learns that God is far above the wisdom of man, and acts to fulfill his own purposes, often testing and allowing the righteous to be afflicted to further perfect them so that they may bring forth much fruit (John 15).

Job 18

Job 18:1 Then answered Bildad the Shuhite, and said, **18:2** How long will it be ere ye make an end of words? mark, and afterwards we will speak.

Bildad asks Job; who are you that God should change his plan on your account, and not punish your wickedness?

18:3 Wherefore are we counted as beasts, and reputed vile in your sight? **18:4** He teareth himself in his anger: shall the earth be forsaken for thee? and shall the rock be removed out of his place? **18:5** Yea, the light of the wicked shall be put out, and the spark of his fire shall not shine.

18:6 The light shall be dark in his [the light of life will fail and he will die] tabernacle, and his candle [properly LAMP, meaning light, life] shall be put out with him.

The wicked will fall in their evil counsel.

18:7 The steps of his strength shall be straitened, and his own counsel shall cast him down. **18:8** For he is cast into a net by his own feet, and he walketh upon a snare. **18:9** The gin shall take him by the heel, and the robber shall prevail against him. **18:10** The snare is laid for him in the ground, and a trap for him in the way.

18:11 Terrors shall make him afraid on every side, and shall drive him to his feet. **18:12** His strength shall be hungerbitten, and destruction shall be ready at his side.

18:13 It [wickedness] shall devour the strength of his skin [flesh]: even the firstborn of death shall devour his strength. **18:14** His confidence shall be rooted out of his tabernacle [tent, body], and it shall bring him to the king of terrors [death itself].

18:15 It [death] shall dwell in his tabernacle [the physical body], because it is none of his [the body is not under our power to live forever, that is the gift of God to the obedient who faithfully live by every Word of God]: brimstone [the lake of fire] shall be scattered upon his habitation.

18:16 His roots shall be dried up beneath, and above shall his branch be cut off. **18:17** His remembrance shall perish from the earth, and he shall have no name in the street.

18:18 He shall be driven from light into darkness, and chased [destroyed from life itself] out of the world.

18:19 He shall neither have son nor nephew among his people, nor any remaining in his dwellings.

This does NOT mean that the wicked will not have family who will repent; it means that being dead and destroyed forever because of unrepentant wickedness; the wicked will be lost to the righteous.

18:20 They that come after him shall be astonied at his day [end], as they that went [lived] before were affrighted [in this life the people are intimidated by the evil power and authority of the wicked].

18:21 Surely such are the dwellings [eternal death is the dwelling of the wicked] of the wicked, and this is the place of him that knoweth not God.

Job 19

Job Answers Bildad's Second Discourse

Job 19:1 Then Job answered and said, **19:2** How long will ye vex my soul, and break me in pieces with words? **19:3** These ten times have ye reproached me: ye are not ashamed that ye make yourselves strange to me.

Job declares that IF he has sinned his friends have not revealed what the sin is; but have only accused him based on his suffering.

19:4 And be it indeed that I have erred, mine error remaineth with myself [unknown to his friends]

Job lists his sufferings and still he is faithful and relies on God. In spite of all he is suffering Job does not sin against God. This is a remarkable statement of faith, loyalty and trust in God during inexplicable suffering.

19:5 If indeed ye will magnify yourselves against me, and plead against me my reproach: **19:6** Know now that God hath overthrown me, and hath compassed me with his net.

19:7 Behold, I cry out of wrong, but I am not heard: I cry aloud, but there is no judgment. **19:8** He hath fenced up my way that I cannot pass, and he hath set darkness in my paths.

19:9 He hath stripped me of my glory, and taken the crown from my head. **19:10** He hath destroyed me on every side, and I am gone: and mine hope hath he removed like a tree.

19:11 He hath also kindled his wrath against me, and he counteth me unto him as one of his enemies. **19:12** His troops come together, and raise up their way against me, and encamp round about my tabernacle.

19:13 He hath put my brethren far from me, and mine acquaintance are verily estranged from me. **19:14** My kinsfolk have failed, and my familiar [closest] friends have forgotten me.

19:15 They that dwell in mine house, and my maids, count me for a stranger: I am an alien in their sight. **19:16** I called my servant, and he gave me no answer; I intreated him with my mouth.

19:17 My breath is strange to my wife, though I intreated for the children's sake of mine own body. **19:18** Yea, young children despised me; I arose, and they spake against me. **19:19** All my inward friends abhorred me: and they whom I loved are turned against me.

19:20 My bone cleaveth to my skin and to my flesh, and I am escaped with the skin of my teeth.

19:21 Have pity upon me, have pity upon me, O ye my friends; for the hand of God hath touched me.

19:22 Why do ye persecute me as God, and are not satisfied with my flesh? **19:23** Oh that my words were now written! oh that they were printed in a

book! **19:24** That they were graven with an iron pen and lead in the rock for ever!

Job maintains his trust in God, in spite of all his afflictions

19:25 For I know that my redeemer liveth, and that he shall stand at the latter day upon the earth: **19:26** And though after my skin worms [I die and maggots] destroy this body, yet in my flesh shall I see God: **19:27** Whom I shall see for myself, and mine eyes shall behold, and not another; though my reins [internal organs] be consumed within me.

Job tells his friends to look to their own state with God instead of judging him because he is afflicted, for they will also face punishment for attacking him in his trials.

19:28 But **ye should say**, Why **persecute we him**, seeing the root of the matter is found in me [Job's friends need to acknowledge that the issue is not in Job but in themselves]? **19:29** Be ye afraid of the sword: for wrath [wrongfully accusing and attacking] bringeth the punishments of the sword, that ye may know there is a judgment.

Hebrews 11 and the faithfulness of the righteous through their sufferings

> **Hebrews 11:1** Now faith is the substance of things hoped for, the evidence of things not seen. **11:2** For by it the elders obtained a good report.

Nineteen hundred years ago Paul spoke of physical things being made from the invisible things; which was confirmed by $E=MC^2$ which means that energy is mass times the speed of light squared or multiplied by itself. The opposite is also true that mass consists of energy. The Creator God who was spirit [pure energy] made matter by converting energy to matter!

Paul understood this by faith; which thing is today confirmed by discovery of the facts. Matter is energy concentrated into matter. Just like ice is a form of water and water is a form of vapor!

> **11:3** Through faith we understand that the worlds were framed by the word of God, so that things which are seen were not made of things which do appear.

> **11:4** By faith Abel offered unto God a more excellent sacrifice than Cain, **by which he obtained witness that he was righteous, God testifying of his gifts**: and by it he being dead yet speaketh.

That is, Abel is dead and yet he is spoken of to this day, and he will be raised up in the resurrection.

> **11:5** By faith Enoch was translated that he should not see death; and was not found, because God had translated him: for before his translation he had this testimony, that he pleased God.

How can we obey God if we do not believe that He exists? and how can we please God [obey Him] if we do not believe he exists?

> **11:6** But without faith it is impossible to please him: for he that cometh to God must believe that he is [exists], and that he is a rewarder of them that diligently seek him.

> **11:7** By faith Noah, being warned of God of things not seen as yet, moved with fear, [believed God and] prepared an ark to the saving of his house; by the which he condemned the world [which would

not believe the warnings], and became heir of the righteousness which is by faith.

This is a lesson, that in the same way those in today's Spiritual Ekklesia who do not believe the warnings and turn to God in sincerity and truth, will also be destroyed.

> **11:8** By faith Abraham, when he was called to go out into a place which he should after receive for an inheritance, **obeyed; and he went out, not knowing whither he went. 11:9** By faith he sojourned in the land of promise, as in a strange country, dwelling in tabernacles [The Feast of Tabernacles requires that we dwell in temporary shelters to make the very point that if we are called and faithful to God, we are strangers in this evil world.] with Isaac and Jacob, the heirs with him of the same promise: **11:10** For he looked for a city which hath foundations, whose builder and maker is God

We are to be focused on the spiritual things of the whole Word of God as Abraham was; and we are to be built on the whole Word of God; which is the Writings, the Prophets and the Apostles [the Holy Scriptures] with Jesus Christ being the Chief Stone of the foundation: All of which were inspired by God!

Abraham believed God and therefore he acted on what God told him to do. To believe God is one thing; to actually act on what God says and to obey him, is something else.

We must believe before we can obey, but if we believe and do not start obeying there is no sacrifice for our sin and there is no reconciliation with God for us.

As long as we continue to reject living by every Word of God, we can believe all we want and it won't do us any good at all. We must believe and then we must act on that belief and start doing what God tells us to do.

Our reconciliation with God and our relationship with Him depends upon us keeping His commandments, and one of those commandments is to honor thy father and thy mother.

In order to keep that commandment, we must be willing to do anything that God the Father tells us to do. Was there any law that said Abraham had to move to a different land? Was there any law that told Noah: by law you have to build this ark? No, there wasn't.

They obeyed the Great Law that says "Honor thy Father and thy mother," which means that we are to live by EVERY Word of God the Father, not just the codified law.

The law is: Obey God in ALL things. We are obligated by the commandment to do what our Father tells us to do, and He told Abraham to leave that land and He told Noah to build that boat.

We are to obey God our Father in whatever He tells us to do. This concept of obedience goes far beyond just the commandments. Yes, we are to keep all of His commandments but we are also to love Him with all our hearts, to serve Him with all our strength and to try and please Him in every way; and that means doing whatever He says, not just what is codified in some written law; always, always, always, at all times.

> **11:11** Through faith also Sara herself received strength to conceive seed, and was delivered of a child when she was past age, because she judged him faithful who had promised. [Where was there any faith in Sarah regarding this promise? She gave herself to her husband Abraham in her old age, trusting that God would give her a son!] **11:12** Therefore sprang there even of one, and him as good as dead, so many as the stars of the sky in multitude, and as the sand which is by the sea shore innumerable.

Out of Sarah and Abraham came a son by God's promise; out of Abram who was a very old man would come as "many as the stars of the sky in multitude, and as the sand which is by the sea shore enumerable.

Now, if they in their great age had not believed that promise, and not added the works of faith to their belief and had not come together; the promise would have been of no effect! The birth of Isaac was by faith in the promise of God, coupled with the works of faith!

Notice they all DIED: which means that Enoch also died. These all died in faith. Enoch was translated that he should not see death; in other words, he was moved from one place to another so that he would not be murdered or killed for his faith at that point, but later on he died;

> **11:13 These all died in faith,** not having received the promises, but having seen them afar off, and were persuaded of them, and embraced them, and confessed that they were strangers and pilgrims on the earth

Those who reject worldliness for godliness, are making a clear statement that they are not of this world and that they seek another and godly nation, the Kingdom of God; and if any turn aside from their zeal to keep the whole Word of God, which is the constitution of the Kingdom of God, and go back into worldliness; they are become worldly again.

> **11:14** For they that say such things declare plainly that they seek a country. **11:15** And truly, if they had been mindful of that country from whence they came out, they might have had opportunity to have returned.

That is the lesson of dwelling in tabernacles or temporary structures at the Feast: To teach us that this flesh is temporary and that we are seeking a better promised land; an eternal spiritual future.

It is to remind us that we are temporary sojourners and foreigners in this society and we must be seeking a better society and a better and spiritual Promised Land, which is found in the Kingdom of God. We are really just temporary sojourners in this flesh; and we should all be looking forward to a better and more permanent place to dwell, a change to spirit and the promise of eternal life. Which is the gift of God for all those who sincerely repent, who turn from sin and commit to sin no more, who are reconciled to God the Father and given His Spirit.

Those who endure and overcome may then be given Eternal life in a new spiritual body at the resurrection when they are changed to spirit. However, right now we are living in this flesh, which is temporary, transitory, it will die. It will decay and we need to find a better way, and that better way is offered by God through Jesus Christ.

> **11:16** But now **they desire a better country, that is, an heavenly: wherefore God is not ashamed to be called their God: for he hath prepared for them** [the faithful who believe and have the works of faith] **a city** [the New Jerusalem].

Abraham had received promises that Isaac would be the father of countless descendants and not understanding the command to kill Isaac when he had those promises, Abraham still obeyed.

> **11:17** By faith Abraham, when he was tried, **offered up Isaac: and he that had received the promises offered up his only begotten son, 11:18** Of whom it was said, **That in Isaac shall thy seed be called: 11:19 Accounting that God was able to raise him up, even from the dead;** from whence also he received him in a figure.

Figuratively speaking, he received Isaac back from the dead, because he was about to kill him and God delivered Isaac.

> **11:20** By faith [in God's promises] Isaac blessed Jacob and Esau concerning things to come. **11:21** By faith [in God's promises] Jacob, when he was a dying, blessed both the sons of Joseph; and worshipped, leaning upon the top of his staff. **11:22** By faith [in

God's promise that he would bring Israel out of Egypt] Joseph, when he died, made mention of the departing of the children of Israel; and gave commandment concerning his bones.

11:23 By faith Moses, when he was born, was hid three months of his parents, because they saw he was a proper child; and they were not afraid of the king's commandment.

11:24 By faith Moses, when he was come to years, refused to be called the son of Pharaoh's daughter; **11:25** Choosing rather to suffer affliction with the people of God, than to enjoy the pleasures of sin for a season; **11:26** Esteeming the reproach of Christ greater riches than the treasures in Egypt: for he had respect unto the recompence of the reward.

Who? Moses esteemed who? Paul showing here that he KNEW that Jesus Christ was the God who was an Husband to Israel under the Mosaic Covenant declares:

By faith in the promise of God, Moses chose to reject Egypt and follow the God of his father Abraham.

11:27 By faith he forsook Egypt, not fearing the wrath of the king: for he endured, as seeing him who is invisible.

Moses obeyed the call of God from the burning bush in Sinai and by faith Moses believed God and killed the Passover in Egypt. It Moses had said I believe and had not had the works of faith in commanding the killing of the lambs; what would have happened to Israel?

11:28 Through faith he kept the passover, and the sprinkling of blood, lest he that destroyed the firstborn should touch them. **11:29** By faith they passed through the Red sea as by dry land: which the Egyptians assaying to do were drowned.

What if Joshua had said, I believe you can do it LORD; and then did not demonstrate his faith with the works of faith and did not march around Jericho?

11:30 By faith the walls of Jericho fell down, after they were compassed about seven days.

What if Rahab had not saved the spies and what if she had not tied the scarlet ribbon [a red ribbon like the red blood of the lambs in Egypt, representing being under the protection of the Lamb of God] to her window? have you ever wondered why a scarlet ribbon? The red ribbon was a type of being under the protection of the blood of the Lamb of God!

11:31 By faith the harlot Rahab perished not with them that believed not, when she had received the spies with peace.

11:32 And what shall I more say? for the time would fail me to tell of Gedeon, and of Barak, and of Samson, and of Jephthae; of David also, and Samuel, and of the prophets: **11:33** Who through faith [and the works of faith, doing mighty deeds in obedience to God] subdued kingdoms, wrought righteousness, obtained promises, stopped the mouths of lions.

11:34 Quenched the violence of fire [Shadrach, Meshach and Abednego], escaped the edge of the sword, out of weakness were made strong, waxed valiant in fight, turned to flight the armies of the aliens.

11:35 Women received their dead raised to life again: and others were tortured, not accepting deliverance; that they might obtain a better resurrection: **11:36** And others had trial of cruel mockings and scourgings, yea, moreover of bonds and imprisonment: **11:37** They were stoned, they were sawn asunder, were tempted, were slain with the sword: they wandered about in sheepskins and goatskins; being destitute, afflicted, tormented; **11:38** (Of whom the world was not worthy:) they wandered in deserts, and in mountains, and in dens and caves of the earth.

All of these faithful called out over the past 6,000 years, who were FULL of the works of Faith died, and now wait in their graves for the promise of the resurrection to eternal life in the Promised Land of eternity! Yet today, so many of the Ekklesia are afraid to take a stand to question and prove the words of men by God's Word; afraid to learn and to keep the whole Word of God; afraid to take a stand against the deceivers and idols of men!

11:39 And these all, having obtained a good report through faith, received not the promise: **11:40** God having provided some better thing for us, that they without us should not be made perfect.

Job 20

Zophar's Second Discourse

Job's friends repeatedly and rightly proclaimed the fate of the wicked and Job agrees with them; yet they sin against Job by accusing the righteous, just because he is suffering and being tested by God.

God has allowed Job to be afflicted to TEST his loyalty to and humility before God, and to perfect his character! Not because of any particular sin of Job's.

Throughout history as it is today, God's elect face continual testing of their loyalty directly to, and humility before God.

The TEST of Job is a continual TEST for ALL of the "called out" of every generation; perhaps in different ways, but the TEST always boils down to our faithful unshakable loyalty to God.

Zophar answers Job's rebuke

Job 20:1 Then answered Zophar the Naamathite, and said, **20:2** Therefore do my thoughts cause me to answer, and for this I make haste. **20:3** I have heard the check of my reproach, and the spirit of my understanding causeth me to answer.

Zophar truthfully speaks of the end of the wicked; and again the false assumption is made that just because someone has trials they must be wicked, when the truth is very different. If God is working with us we will have trials to purge us and prune us so that we might bring forth much fruit of godliness.

Neither trials nor blessings are proof of godliness in this life, for Satan persecutes the righteous and blesses the wicked within the limits set by God for our own good.

The sole proof of a good relationship with God is the degree of zeal we have for the practical KEEPING, for OBEDIENCE; to live by every Word of God; which is love personified! We are to be as faithful as faithful Abraham or faithful Job in all our blessings and all OUR TRIALS.

20:4 Knowest thou not this of old, since man was placed upon earth, **20:5** That the triumphing of the wicked is short, and the joy of the hypocrite but for a moment? **20:6** Though his excellency mount up to the heavens, and his head reach unto the clouds; **20:7** Yet he shall perish for ever like his own dung: they which have seen him shall say, Where is he? **20:8** He shall fly away as a dream, and shall not be found: yea, he shall be chased away as a vision of the night.

The wicked who break any of God's commandments willfully if they remain unrepentant, will be destroyed by Christ and shall be no more.

20:9 The eye also which saw him shall see him no more; neither shall his place any more behold him. **20:10** His children shall seek to please the poor, and his hands shall restore their goods.

The unrepentant wicked shall be destroyed even if they prosper for a time.

20:11 His bones are full of the sin of his youth, which shall lie down with him in the dust. **20:12** Though wickedness be sweet in his mouth, though he hide it under his tongue; **20:13** Though he spare it, and forsake it not; but keep it still within his mouth: **20:14** Yet his meat [wickedness] in his bowels is turned, it is the gall of asps within him.

Wealth and gain gotten by wickedness shall be taken away from the unrepentant.

20:15 He hath swallowed down riches, and he shall vomit them up again: God shall cast them out of his belly. **20:16** He shall suck the poison of asps: the viper's tongue shall slay him. **20:17** He shall not see the rivers, the floods, the brooks of honey and butter.

20:18 That which he laboured for shall he restore [give back], and shall not swallow it down: according to his substance shall the restitution be, and he shall not rejoice therein.

The wicked shall fear that other wicked folks will take their evil gains and they shall have much stress and worry.

20:19 Because he hath oppressed and hath forsaken the poor; because he hath violently taken away an house which he builded not; **20:20** Surely he shall not feel quietness in his belly, he shall not save of that which he desired. **20:21** There shall none of his meat [food] be left; therefore shall no man look for his goods.

God shall bring the wicked down, no matter how great or prosperous they are.

20:22 In the fulness of his sufficiency he shall be in straits: every hand of the wicked shall come upon him. **20:23** When he is about to fill his belly, God shall cast the fury of his wrath upon him, and shall rain it upon him while he is eating.

God will allow the enemy to strike down the wicked in the coming great tribulation of correction on the Church of God.

20:24 He shall flee from the iron [powerful] weapon, and the bow of steel shall strike him through.

The wicked will be pierced through for their pride and compromising with the Word of God.

20:25 It is drawn, and cometh out of the body; yea, the glittering sword cometh out of his gall: terrors are upon him.

An uncontrolled unstoppable fire of correction will sweep over the wicked and the wicked who survive will suffer much.

20:26 All darkness shall be hid in his secret places: a fire not blown shall consume him; it shall go ill with him that is left in his tabernacle [body].

Of a truth, this is the portion of the unrepentant brethren in today's Spiritual Ekklesia who refuse to repent of exalting traditions, men and organizations above the Word of God; who continue in Sabbath and High Day pollution and in their many other sins!

Almighty God shall judge us for our iniquity and lukewarmness to live by his Word. Christ shall cast those not burning with zeal for his commandments out of his body and into great affliction in the hope that we will repent; for we have been judged and found lacking in the loyalty of Job!

Revelation 3:14 And unto the angel of the church of the Laodiceans write; These things saith the Amen, the faithful and true witness, the beginning of the creation of God;

Laodicea is HOT for their traditions, leaders and organizations, and COLD, devoid of zeal for practical obedience to God's Word; this mixture results in lukewarmness before Christ.

3:15 I know thy works, that thou art neither cold nor hot: I would thou wert cold or hot.

3:16 So then because thou art lukewarm, and neither cold nor hot, I will spue thee out of my mouth.

We are arrogant and full of pride and no one can tell us anything; we are "know it all's", not understanding how very little we really know and how spiritually blind and naked of righteousness we are before Christ.

3:17 Because thou sayest, I am rich, and increased with goods, and have need of nothing; and knowest not that thou art wretched, and miserable, and poor, and blind, and naked:

Seek the true spiritual gold of God's Word because our physical wealth will be destroyed in the fire of tribulation: Seek the righteousness of zeal to live by every Word of God in sincere repentance, so that our shameful sins may be covered by the sacrifice of Christ and we may be clothed in godly righteousness. Seek the Spirit of God through zeal to live by every Word of God, so that our eyes may be opened to understanding the things of God.

3:18 I counsel thee to buy of me gold tried in the fire, that thou mayest be rich; and white raiment, that thou mayest be clothed, and that the shame of thy nakedness do not appear; and anoint thine eyes with eyesalve, that thou mayest see.

We will be rejected until we sincerely repent and turn back to seek our God; because Christ loves us so much he will afflict the flesh to save the spirit for eternity.

3:19 As many as I love, I rebuke and chasten: be zealous therefore, and repent.

If we do repent and open our mind to Christ, keeping God's commandments with righteous zeal; he will receive us and teach us the ways of godliness.

3:20 Behold, I stand at the door, and knock: if any man hear my voice, and open the door, I will come in to him, and will sup with him, and he with me.

If we overcome our lukewarmness for the practical keeping of all of God's Word; if we will overcome the idolatry of exalting men, traditions and organizations above God and his law: then we shall be saved and rise up to sit with Christ in his government in the Kingdom of God.

3:21 To him that overcometh will I grant to sit with me in my throne, even as I also overcame, and am set down with my Father in his throne.

Job 20:27 The heaven shall reveal his iniquity; and the earth shall rise up against him.

The unrepentant wicked who compromise with any part of God's Word will be destroyed.

20:28 The increase of his house shall depart, and his goods shall flow away in the day of his wrath.

20:29 This is the portion of a wicked man from God, and the heritage appointed unto him by God.

Job 21

Job Answers Zophar

Job 21:1 But Job answered and said, **21:2** Hear diligently my speech, and let this be your consolations. **21:3** Suffer me that I may speak; and after that I have spoken, mock on.

Job asks the question, why do the righteous suffer and the wicked are blessed?

21:4 As for me, is my complaint to man? and if it were so, why should not my spirit be troubled? **21:5** Mark me, and be astonished, and lay your hand upon your mouth.

21:6 Even when I remember [the fate of the wicked] I am afraid, and trembling taketh hold on my flesh [we must learn to loath sin].

21:7 Wherefore do the wicked live, become [to an old age] old, yea, are mighty in power? **21:8** Their seed is established in their sight with them, and their offspring before their eyes.

21:9 Their houses are safe from fear, neither is the rod of God upon them. **21:10** Their bull gendereth [cattle reproduce], and faileth not; their cow calveth, and casteth not her calf. **21:11** They send forth their little ones like a flock, and their children dance.

The wicked rejoice and party in their sins, as they reject God's Word for their own ways.

21:12 They take the timbrel and harp, and rejoice at the sound of the organ. **21:13** They spend their days in wealth, and in a moment go down to the grave.

21:14 Therefore they say unto God, Depart from us; for we desire not the knowledge of thy ways. **21:15** What is the Almighty, that we should serve him? and what profit should we have, if we pray unto him?

Job will have NO part in wickedness and sin.

21:16 Lo, their good is not in their hand [their ultimate end is not under their control and the godly despise the ways of the wicked]: the counsel of the wicked is far from me.

Job knows that the end of the commandment breaker is their destruction. It is vital to look at the end of the matter and not at the middle of it.

21:17 How oft is the candle of the wicked put out! and how oft cometh their destruction upon them! God distributeth sorrows in his anger. **21:18** They are as stubble before the wind, and as chaff that the storm carrieth away. **21:19** God layeth up his iniquity [remembers] for his children [if they do not repent]: he rewardeth him, and he [the wicked shall know the destruction of God for their sins] shall know it. **21:20** His eyes shall see his destruction, and he shall drink of the wrath of the Almighty.

The wicked have their pleasures for a very short time now and shall have no pleasure in their future of eternal death; while the righteous shall inherit eternal life.

21:21 For what pleasure hath he in his house [grave] after him, when the number of his months is cut off [after he dies] in the midst?

Is any man as wise as God? Can any man teach God any thing?

21:22 Shall any teach God knowledge? seeing he judgeth those that are high.

Both the wealthy and the afflicted shall die and lie in the grave.

21:23 One dieth in his full strength, being wholly at ease and quiet. **21:24** His breasts are full of milk, and his bones are moistened with marrow.

21:25 And another dieth in the bitterness of his soul, and never eateth with pleasure.

21:26 They shall lie down alike in the dust, and the worms shall cover them.

21:27 Behold, I know your thoughts, and the devices which ye wrongfully imagine against me.

The wicked who compromise with or break God's Word, may be exalted for a time to TEST the godly; but the unrepentant wicked are reserved for God's day to be judge and destroyed in the fire.

21:28 For ye say, Where is the house of the prince? and where are the dwelling places of the wicked? **21:29** Have ye not asked them that go by the way? and do ye not know their tokens, **21:30 That the wicked is reserved to the day of destruction? they shall be brought forth to the day of wrath.**

Even if no man can resist a wicked ruler; in the end even the most powerful ruler shall surely perish.

21:31 Who shall declare his way to his face? and who shall repay himwhat he hath done? **21:32** Yet shall he be brought to the grave, and shall remain in the tomb.

21:33 The clods [the grave shall give rest] of the valley shall be sweet unto him, and every [all people shall die alike] man shall draw after him, as there are innumerable before him.

Job asks: Why do you seek to comfort me by counting me among the wicked?

21:34 How then comfort ye me in vain, seeing in your answers there remaineth falsehood?

Job 22

Eliphaz: Third Discourse

Eliphaz lists the deeds and the end of the wicked, and then accuses Job of sin. Job responds by saying that he well knows the deeds and the end of the wicked, and has therefore kept himself from sin.

Eliphaz asks: What is a man that God is mindful of him? He then goes on to accuse Job of wickedness and encourages him to repent.

Job 22:1 Then Eliphaz the Temanite answered and said, **22:2** Can a man be profitable unto God, as he that is wise may be profitable unto himself? **22:3** Is it any pleasure to the Almighty, that thou art righteous? or is it gain to him, that thou makest thy ways perfect? **22:4** Will he reprove thee for fear of thee? will he enter with thee into judgment?

One form of wickedness is to fail to help the needy. Eliphaz accuses Job of caring nothing for the poor while respecting the great.

22:5 Is not thy wickedness great? and thine iniquities infinite? **22:6** For thou hast taken a pledge from thy brother for nought, and stripped the naked of their clothing. **22:7** Thou hast not given water to the weary to drink, and thou hast withholden bread from the hungry.

Job is accused of respecting the mighty and rejecting the poor.

22:8 But as for the mighty man, he had [possesses] the earth; and the honourable man dwelt in it. **22:9** Thou hast sent widows away empty, and the arms [strength of the orphans] of the fatherless have been broken.

Respecters of persons will be corrected by God.

22:10 Therefore snares are round about thee, and sudden fear troubleth thee; **22:11** Or darkness, that thou canst not see; and abundance of waters cover thee.

How can sin be hid from the awesome God?

22:12 Is not God in the height of heaven? and behold the height of the stars, how high they are! **22:13** And thou sayest, How doth God know? can he judge through the dark cloud? **22:14** Thick clouds are a covering to him, that he seeth not; and he walketh in the circuit of heaven.

Eliphaz reminds Job of the pre-flood world, and how the wicked were blessed until God destroyed them with the great flood.

22:15 Hast thou marked the old way which wicked men have trodden? **22:16** Which were cut down out of time, **whose foundation was overflown with a flood: 22:17** Which said unto God, Depart from us: and what can the Almighty do for them? **22:18** Yet he filled their houses with good things: but the counsel of the wicked is far from me [Eliphaz].

The righteous are glad that wickedness is destroyed; for the sorrows that wickedness brings are also destroyed.

22:19 The righteous see it, and are glad: and the innocent laugh them to scorn.

The wicked will be consumed in the fire, but the righteous shall remain forever

22:20 Whereas our substance [of the righteous] is not cut down, but the remnant of them [the wicked] the fire consumeth.

22:21 Acquaint now thyself with him [repent and reconcile with God], and be at peace: thereby good shall come unto thee. **22:22** Receive, I pray thee, the law from his mouth, and lay up his words in thine heart.

22:23 If thou return to the Almighty, thou shalt be built up, thou shalt put away iniquity far from thy tabernacles. **22:24** Then shalt thou lay up gold as dust, and the gold of Ophir as the stones of the brooks. **22:25** Yea, the

Almighty shall be thy defence, and thou shalt have plenty of silver. **22:26** For then shalt thou have thy delight in the Almighty, and shalt lift up thy face unto God.

22:27 Thou shalt make thy prayer unto him, and he shall hear thee, and thou shalt pay thy vows [our baptismal marriage vow to obey all that comes out of the mouth of our Husband, Jesus Christ; who instructs us to live by every Word of God] .

22:28 Thou shalt also decree a thing, and it shall be established unto thee: and the light shall shine upon thy ways. **22:29** When men are cast down, then thou shalt say, There is [also a] lifting up; and he shall save the humble person.

The innocent [of failing to live by every Word of God] will be delivered; even if they are standing alone as an island of godliness in a sea of wickedness.

22:30 He shall deliver the island of the innocent: and it is delivered by the pureness of thine hands.

Job 23

Job Responds

Like all godly people, Job complains of the false judgment of men and longs for the righteous judgment of God.

Job 23:1 Then Job answered and said, **23:2** Even to day is my complaint bitter: my stroke is heavier than my groaning. **23:3** Oh that I knew where I might find him [God] ! that I might come even to his seat! **23:4** I would order my cause before him, and fill my mouth with arguments.

Job seeks understanding from God concerning his condition and its cause.

23:5 I would know the words which he would answer me, and understand what he would say unto me.

Job declares that God would strengthen him to understand and would judge him righteously so that he will be delivered from the wicked.

23:6 Will he plead against me with his great power? No; but he would put strength in me.

Job is repentant and wants God to reveal to him his faults and to explain how he may be reconciled to God.

23:7 There the righteous might dispute [reason] with him [God]; so should I be delivered for ever from my judge [from those that judge me falsely].

Job seeks God and deliverance.

23:8 Behold, I go forward, but he is not there; and backward, but I cannot perceive him: **23:9** On the left hand, where he doth work, but I cannot behold him: he hideth himself on the right hand, that I cannot see him:

Job knows that God knows that Job has not sinned, and that God is TESTING him and refining him. Job has been absolutely faithful and loyal to God in spite of all his TESTING.

23:10 But he knoweth the way that I take: when he hath tried me, I shall come forth as gold. **23:11** My foot hath held his steps, his way have I kept, and not declined. **23:12** Neither have I gone back from the commandment of his lips; I have esteemed the words of his mouth more than my necessary food.

God is able to do whatever God wills, and God performs his will towards men.

23:13 But he is in one mind, and who can turn him? and **what his soul desireth, even that he doeth. 23:14** For **he performeth the thing that is appointed for me**: and many such things are with him.

People should fear the greatness and power of God.

23:15 Therefore am I troubled at his presence: when I consider, I am afraid of him.

God softens the hardness of men's hearts through his mighty deeds, bringing men to sincere repentance so that God may give the gift of a soft teachable heart through his Spirit, by which God may write all of his Word on a heart of flesh and not of stone (Ezek 36:26, Jer 31).

23:16 For God maketh my heart soft, and the Almighty troubleth [humbles] me:

Because God allowed Job to live through those dark days, and afflicted Job with this dark sorrow; Job's heart has cleaved to God even more.

23:17 Because I was not cut off before the darkness, neither hath he covered the darkness from my face.

Job 24

Since God knows all things, why do men seek to hide sin?

Job 24:1 Why, seeing times [events] are not hidden from the Almighty, do they that know him not see his days? [walk in his light]

The deeds of the wicked are seen by God; and their end in God's righteous judgment is sure destruction. I know this, says Job [even as we also know it]; therefore I have not sinned before God.

24:2 Some remove the landmarks [like modern Judah Hos 5:10]; they violently take away flocks, and feed [eat them] up thereof. **24:3** They drive away the ass of the fatherless, they take the widow's ox for a pledge. **24:4** They turn the needy out of the way: the poor of the earth hide themselves together.

24:5 Behold, as [like] wild asses in the desert, go they [the wicked go] forth to their work; rising betimes for [to seek out] a prey: the wilderness yieldeth food for them and for their children. **24:6** They reap every one his corn [grain] in the field: and they gather the vintage [advantages] of the wicked.

24:7 They cause the naked to lodge without clothing, that they have no covering in the cold. **24:8** They [the poor, victims of the wicked] are wet with the showers of the mountains, and embrace the rock for want [lack of] of a shelter.

24:9 They pluck the fatherless from the breast [take away the sustenance of the widow and the fatherless], and take a pledge of the poor. **24:10** They cause him to go naked without clothing, and they take away the sheaf [of grain, food] from the hungry; **24:11** Which [the poor] make oil within their walls, and tread their winepresses, and [have it taken from them] suffer thirst.

24:12 [Innocent]Men groan from out of the city, and the soul of the wounded crieth out: yet God layeth not folly to them.

24:13 They are of those that rebel against the light [Word of God]; they know not the ways [of God] thereof, nor abide in the paths [of God] thereof.

24:14 The murderer rising with the light killeth the poor and needy, and [goes out into] in the night is as a thief. **24:15** The eye also of the adulterer waiteth for the twilight, saying, No eye shall see me: and disguiseth his face.

24:16 In the dark they dig through [burgle] houses, which they had marked for themselves in the daytime: they know not the light [God].

The wicked fear the exposure of the light, therefore they seek to keep all their doings secret and are furious when their evil deeds are exposed.

24:17 For the morning is to them even as the shadow of death: if one know them, they are in the terrors of the shadow of death.

There is nothing hidden to God and he will ultimately expose all the wicked with all their unrepentant sins. In his own good time God will judge and repay the wicked for all their evil deeds.

24:18 He [God] is swift as the waters [a rushing stream]; their portion is cursed in the earth: he beholdeth not the way of the vineyards. **24:19** Drought and heat consume the snow waters: so doth the grave those which have sinned.

24:20 The womb shall forget [the unrepentant wicked shall ultimately be forgotten by their own mothers] him; the worm [maggot] shall feed sweetly on him; he shall be no more remembered; and wickedness shall be broken as a tree.

24:21 He [the wicked] evil entreateth the barren that beareth not: and doeth not good to the widow.

24:22 He draweth [deceives and entices] also the mighty with his [evil] power: he [the wicked] riseth up, and no man is sure of life [all fear for their possessions and lives].

Even though the wicked live prosperously and safe for a time, the eyes of God are upon them, watching and judging them.

24:23 Though it be given him [the wicked] to be in safety, whereon he resteth; yet his [God's] eyes are upon their ways [the deeds of the wicked].

24:24 They [the wicked] are exalted for a little while, but are gone and brought low; they are taken out of the way as all other, and cut off as the tops of the ears of corn [grain, the wicked are cut off from the harvest into God's gift of eternal life].

Job insists that this is the truth. He answers his friend by saying that he knows that this is the truth and that knowing this, Job has been faithful to God and not done wickedly.

24:25 And if it be not so now, who will make me a liar, and make my speech nothing worth?

Job 25

Bildad's Third Discourse

Bildad continues his argument that Job has sinned, by asking Job if he can resist God.

Job 25-28 is about the wisdom and power of God.

Job 25:1 Then answered Bildad the Shuhite, and said, **25:2** Dominion and fear are with him [God], he [God] maketh peace in his high places.

25:3 Is there any number of his [any limit to God's strength?] armies? and upon whom doth not his light arise? **25:4** How then can man be justified with God? or how can he be clean that is born of a woman? **25:5** Behold even to [God established the course of the moon from full to darkness] the moon, and it shineth not; yea, the stars are not pure in his sight.

25:6 How much less [a man is so much less than God] man, that is a worm [maggot]? and the son of man, which is a worm [maggot]?

Job 26

Job Responds

Job agrees that God is mighty and asks: Can you help a man against God? Can any man resist God? Job speaks of the might and wisdom of God; insisting that he would not sin against God.

Job 26:1 But Job answered and said, **26:2** How hast thou helped him that is without power? how savest thou the arm that hath no strength? **26:3** How hast thou counselled him that hath no wisdom? and how hast thou plentifully declared the thing as it is? **26:4** To whom hast thou uttered words? and whose spirit came from thee? **26:5** Dead things are formed from under the waters, and the inhabitants thereof.

26:6 Hell is naked before him [God], and destruction hath no [place to hide] covering. **26:7** He stretcheth out the north over the empty place, and hangeth the earth upon nothing. **26:8** He bindeth up the waters in his thick clouds; and the cloud is not rent [cloud does not collapse from the sky by the weight of the water] under them.

God hides the place of his throne from men.

26:9 He holdeth back the face of his throne, and spreadeth his cloud upon it.

God has made the dry land to rise above the waters.

26:10 He hath compassed the waters with bounds, until the day and night come to an end.

The heavenly bodies are maintained by God's power and shake at God's Word.

26:11 The pillars of heaven tremble and are astonished at his reproof.

God has made the dry land to divide the sea; shall he not humble the proud commandments breakers who lean to the pathetic wisdom of mortal man.

26:12 He divideth the sea with his power, and by his understanding he smiteth through the proud.

God created the heavens and all that lives on the earth.

26:13 By his spirit he hath garnished the heavens; his hand hath formed the crooked serpent.

We have heard only a tiny part of the greatness of God; who can understand God's wisdom and might?

26:14 Lo, these are parts of his ways: but how little a portion is heard of him? but the thunder of his power who can understand?

Job 27

Job continues to exalt God even as he suffers; demonstrating his loyalty is not predicated on blessings, but is absolute during both blessings and sorrows.

Job 27:1 Moreover Job continued his parable [teaching], and said, **27:2** As God liveth, who hath taken away my judgment; and the Almighty, who hath vexed my soul;

27:3 All the while [as long as I live] **my breath is in me, and the spirit of God is in my nostrils; 27:4 My lips shall not speak wickedness, nor my tongue utter deceit.**

27:5 God forbid that I should justify you [by agreeing that God has been unjust, or that I have sinned against him]: till I die I will not remove mine integrity from me. **27:6** My righteousness I hold fast, and will not let it go: my heart shall not reproach me so long as I live.

27:7 Let mine enemy be [my adversary [who is really Satan] be destroyed] as the wicked, and he that riseth up against me as the unrighteous.

Job will not be a hypocrite by refusing to do what he has taught others to do.

27:8 For what is the hope of the hypocrite, though he hath gained [much], when God taketh away his soul [life]? **27:9** Will God hear his cry when trouble cometh upon him? **27:10** Will he delight himself in the Almighty? will he always call upon God? **27:11** I will teach you by the hand of God: that which is with the Almighty will I not conceal.

Every wise man knows that the wicked will be destroyed. Job has taught this and now his friends try to teach Job what they had previously learned from him.

27:12 Behold, all ye yourselves have seen it; why then are ye thus altogether vain? **27:13** This is the portion of a wicked man with God, and the heritage of oppressors, which they shall receive of the Almighty.

More on the end of the wicked

27:14 If his [unrepentant] children be multiplied, it is for the sword: and his offspring shall not be satisfied with bread.

27:15 Those that remain of [the wicked] him shall be buried in death: and his [their] widows shall not weep [the end of their oppression].

Ultimately the just shall inherit the earth, and the unrepentant wicked shall inherit destruction.

27:16 Though he heap up silver as the dust, and prepare raiment as the clay; **27:17** He may prepare it, but the just shall put it on, and the innocent shall divide the silver. **27:18** He buildeth his house as a moth, and as a booth that the keeper maketh. **27:19** The rich man shall lie down, but he shall not [enjoy his riches] be gathered: he openeth his eyes, and he is not [dies].

Fears come up against the wicked like the continual lapping of the waves; and he has his sleep disturbed in the night.

27:20 Terrors take hold on him as waters, a tempest stealeth him away in the night. **27:21** The east wind carrieth him away, and he departeth: and as a storm hurleth him out of his place.

The wicked will flee from God's correction, and the repentant righteous will reject the evil doer.

27:22 For God shall cast upon him, and not spare: he would fain flee out of his hand. **27:23** Men shall clap their hands at him, and shall hiss him out of his place.

Job 28

The Greatness of God

God has created the earth and all its wealth and beauty. This chapter is about the great power and wisdom of God: Why should mankind, especially called out people; be tempted to compromise with any part of God's Word of wisdom and life?

Job 28:1 Surely there is a vein for the silver, and a place for gold where they fine it. **28:2** Iron is taken out of the earth, and brass is molten out of the stone. **28:3** He [God] setteth an end to darkness [with the dawn; and enlightens the ignorant], and searcheth out all perfection: the stones of darkness, and the shadow of death.

Even the waters are controlled by God, so that God may take them away if he so wills.

28:4 The flood breaketh out from the inhabitant; even the waters forgotten of the foot [foot peddle powered irrigation]: they are dried up, they are gone away from men.

Job knows that the center of the earth is a fire; the ancients knew far more than some think.

28:5 As for the earth, out of it cometh bread: and under it is turned up as it were fire.

Precious stones are hidden in the earth, all made by God.

28:6 The stones of it are the place of sapphires: and it hath dust of gold.

God knows even the most secret things.

28:7 There is a path which no fowl knoweth, and which the vulture's eye hath not seen: **28:8** The lion's whelps have not trodden it, nor the fierce lion passed by it.

God has the wisdom and power to resurface the earth if he so desires.

28:9 He putteth forth his hand upon the rock; he overturneth the mountains by the roots. **28:10** He cutteth out rivers among the rocks; and his eye seeth every precious thing. **28:11** He bindeth the floods [God sets the seas and bodies of water to their places] from overflowing; and the thing that is hid bringeth he forth to light.

God is full of wisdom, but there is no godly wisdom in man. Man NEEDS the gift of spiritual wisdom from God.

28:12 But where shall wisdom be found? and where is the place of understanding? **28:13** Man knoweth not the price thereof; neither is it found in the land of the living. **28:14** The depth saith, It is not in me: and the sea saith, It is not with me.

Godly wisdom cannot be purchased for money; it must be acquired by learning, assimilating, submitting to and living by every Word of God

28:15 It cannot be gotten for gold, neither shall silver be weighed for the price thereof. **28:16** It cannot be valued with the gold of Ophir, with the precious onyx, or the sapphire. **28:17** The gold and the crystal cannot equal it: and the exchange of it shall not be for jewels of fine gold. **28:18** No mention shall be made of coral, or of pearls: for the price of wisdom is above rubies. **28:19** The topaz of Ethiopia shall not equal it, neither shall it be valued with pure gold.

28:20 Whence then cometh wisdom? and where is the place of understanding? **28:21** Seeing it is hid from the eyes of all living, and kept close [hidden] from the fowls of the air. **28:22** Destruction and death say, We have heard the fame thereof with our ears [but we know it not].

True wisdom is of God and begins with R E S P E C T for God and diligently learning and living by every Word of God.

Psalm 111:10 The fear of the Lord is the beginning of wisdom: a good understanding have all they that do his commandments: his praise endureth for ever.

Job 28:23 God understandeth the way thereof, and he knoweth the place thereof. **28:24** For he [God] looketh to the ends of the earth, and seeth under the whole heaven; **28:25** To make the weight for the winds; and he weigheth the waters by measure.

God created all things by his wisdom

28:26 When he made a decree for the rain, and a way for the lightning of the thunder: **28:27** Then did he see it, and declare it; he prepared it, yea, and searched it out.

28:28 And unto man he said, Behold, the fear of the LORD, that is wisdom; and to depart from evil [by obeying God] is understanding.

Job 29

Job Declares his Zeal for God

Job rehearses the story of his life, his prosperity and his trials

Job 29:1 Moreover Job continued his parable, and said, **29:2** Oh that I were as in months past, as in the days when God preserved me; **29:3** When [God smiled and blessed me] his candle shined upon my head, and when by his light I walked through darkness; **29:4** As I was in the days of my youth, when the secret [wisdom of the Word of God] of God was upon my tabernacle [life];

29:5 When the Almighty was yet with me, when my children were about me; **29:6** When I washed my steps with butter, and the rock poured me out rivers of oil; **29:7** When I went out to the gate through the city, when I prepared my seat in the street! **29:8** The young men saw me, and hid themselves [were humble and respectful before me]: and the aged arose [in respect for me], and stood up.

Job recounts that even the rulers respected the wisdom of God's Word which was given to him for his zealous faithfulness.

29:9 The princes refrained talking, and laid their hand on their mouth. **29:10** The nobles held their peace, and their tongue cleaved to the roof of their mouth.

Those who saw and heard Job and his teachings, blessed him for the deliverance that God's Word brings.

29:11 When the ear heard me, then it blessed me; and when the eye saw me, it gave witness to me: **29:12** Because I delivered the poor that cried, and the fatherless, and him that had none to help him.

Those who were delivered by the Word of God which was taught by Job, blessed him; and the poor and widows rejoiced in his help as he applied God's Word in all he did.

29:13 The blessing of him that was ready to perish came upon me: and I caused the widow's heart to sing for joy.

God's commandments are righteousness and love; and Job put them on like a garment

29:14 I put on righteousness, and it clothed me: my judgment was as a robe and a diadem.

The commandments of God give sight [wisdom] to the [spiritually] blind and strength to the spiritually weak.

29:15 I was eyes to the blind, and feet was I to the lame.

God is a Father to the poor in spirit who exalt him and do his will, and Job by doing the Father's will was like a father to his people.

> **Matthew 5:2** And he opened his mouth, and taught them, saying,
>
> **5:3** Blessed are the poor in spirit: for theirs is the kingdom of heaven.
>
> **5:4** Blessed are they that mourn: for they shall be comforted.
>
> **5:5** Blessed are the meek: for they shall inherit the earth.
>
> **5:6** Blessed are they which do hunger and thirst after righteousness: for they shall be filled.
>
> **5:7** Blessed are the merciful: for they shall obtain mercy.
>
> **5:8** Blessed are the pure in heart: for they shall see God.
>
> **5:9** Blessed are the peacemakers: for they shall be called the children of God.
>
> **5:10** Blessed are they which are persecuted for righteousness' sake: for theirs is the kingdom of heaven.

5:11 Blessed are ye, when men shall revile you, and persecute you, and shall say all manner of evil against you falsely, for my sake.

5:12 Rejoice, and be exceeding glad: for great is your reward in heaven: for so persecuted they the prophets which were before you.

Job delivered the poor and was like a father to them, searching out the true justice of any cause as a godly judge.

Job 29:16 I was a father to the poor: and the cause which I knew not I searched out.

The commandments of God are wisdom and deliver men out of the mouth of destruction [ultimately delivering from death itself].

29:17 And I brake the jaws of the wicked, and plucked the spoil out of his teeth.

Job believed that he would never suffer any ill because he was faithful and righteous before God; not understanding that God also TESTS and purges the faithful so that they may bear even more fruit (john 15).

29:18 Then I said, I shall die in my nest [his own home surrounded by his children at a old age], and I shall multiply my days as the sand.

Job was rich and full of Godly wisdom because of his faithfulness to God. Wisdom brought him wealth and the respect of all around him.

29:19 My root was spread out by the waters, and the dew lay all night upon my branch. **29:20** My glory was fresh in me, and my bow [strength] was renewed in my hand. **29:21** Unto me men gave ear, and waited, and kept silence [did not interrupt] at my counsel. **29:22** After my words they spake not again [did not answer back]; and my speech dropped upon them. **29:23** And they waited for me as for the rain; and they opened their mouth wide as for the latter rain.

Job was strong like a well watered fruitful tree.

29:24 If I laughed on them, they believed it not; and the light of my countenance they cast not down.

Men did not believe that Job could make any mistake and rejoiced at his appearing.

29:25 I chose out their way, and sat chief, and dwelt as a king in the army, as one that comforteth the mourners.

Job was a mighty, wise and godly man, a leader of the people.

Job 30

Job's Test of Suffering

Job 30:1 But now they that are younger than I have me in derision, whose fathers I would have disdained to have set with the dogs of my flock.

Job complains, I was old and respected for wisdom, now because of my trial even the foolish young men despise me.

30:2 Yea, whereto might the strength of their hands profit me, in whom old age was perished?

What profit is there in the physical strength of many servants and riches when we are dying?

Foolish young men who were in deep poverty because of their foolishness now condemn Job who was wise, because of his calamities.

30:3 For want and famine they were solitary; fleeing into the wilderness in former time desolate and waste. **30:4** Who cut up mallows [swamp greens] by the bushes, and juniper roots for their meat. **30:5** They were driven forth from among men, (they cried after them as after a thief;) **30:6** To dwell in the cliffs of the valleys, in caves of the earth, and in the rocks. **30:7** Among the bushes they brayed; under the nettles they were gathered together. **30:8** They were children of fools, yea, children of base men: they were viler than the earth.

Job is despised by even these sons of Belial, who now spit in Job's face and say that he who taught godliness is a hypocrite and sinner.

30:9 And now am I their song, yea, I am their byword. **30:10** They abhor me, they flee far from me, and spare not to spit in my face.

Because God has afflicted him and loosed his blessings from Job; the foolish wicked have loosed off their self-restraint and poured out abuse towards Job.

30:11 Because he hath loosed my cord, and afflicted me, they have also let loose the bridle before me. **30:12** Upon my right hand rise the youth; they push away [seek to cause me to stumble in my loyalty to God] my feet, and they raise up against me the ways of their destruction.

When the faithful are TESTED and suffer they are mocked by the wicked; who call the zealous fools and say: "What is the profit in serving God?" The wicked, lax and lukewarm, attack the zealous for God when they are in their trials. They are motivated by Satan to add mockery to the pain and so entice people to say "There is no profit in zeal for God" and tempt them to turn away from God.

30:13 They mar my path, they set forward my calamity, they have no helper. **30:14** They came upon me as a wide breaking in of waters [as from a broken dam]: in the desolation [of the righteous, they add to sorrows] they rolled themselves upon me.

Job's fears have come upon him.

30:15 Terrors are turned upon me: they pursue my soul as the wind: and my welfare passeth away as a cloud. **30:16** And now my soul [my life] is poured out upon me; the days of affliction have taken hold upon me. **30:17** My bones are pierced in me in the night season: and my sinews take no rest.

Job's body is swollen.

30:18 By the great force of my disease is my garment changed: it bindeth me about as the collar of my coat. **30:19** He hath cast me into the mire, and I am become like dust and ashes.

Job begs for mercy and it is delayed.

30:20 I cry unto thee [God], and thou dost not hear me: I stand up, and thou regardest me not. **30:21** Thou art become cruel to me: with thy strong hand thou opposest thyself against me.

30:22 Thou liftest me up to the wind; thou causest me to ride upon it [be blown about in thoughts], and dissolvest my substance.

Unto all men death is appointed once.

30:23 For I know that thou wilt bring me to death, and to the house appointed for all living.

Job, not yet knowing of the plan of salvation [revealed by Christ] considers that this physical life may be all there is.

30:24 Howbeit he will not stretch out his hand to the grave, though they cry in his destruction.

Job had been concerned for the afflicted and now seeks God's concern for his own affliction.

30:25 Did not I weep for him that was in trouble? was not my soul grieved for the poor? **30:26** When I looked for good, then evil came unto me: and when I waited for light, there came darkness.

Job sorrows night and day, and suffers abdominal distress in his agony of spirit.

30:27 My bowels boiled, and rested not: the days of affliction prevented me. **30:28** I went mourning without the sun: I stood up, and I cried in the congregation.

Job says that he is like a wandering wild beast having lost his home and wealth.

30:29 I am a brother to dragons, and a companion to owls. **30:30** My skin is black [sunburned and dried out] upon me, and my bones are burned with heat.

30:31 My harp [songs of joy] also is turned to mourning, and my organ into the voice of them that weep.

Job 31

A list of sins and their consequences; each of which has its spiritual application.

Job covenanted with a wife and was faithful to her; this is analogous of our marriage covenant with Jesus Christ our espoused Husband.

Job 31:1 I made a covenant with mine eyes [to desire only my spouse]; why then should I think upon a maid?

The end of covenant breakers; who break their marriage covenant with Christ to do all that he requires; which is to live by every Word of God: is destruction. While the righteous will be lifted up to the marriage feast and eternal life in unity with Messiah the Christ and God the Father.

31:2 For what portion of God is there from above? and what inheritance of the Almighty from on high? **31:3** Is not destruction to the wicked? and a strange punishment to the workers of iniquity? **31:4** Doth not he see my ways, and count all my steps? **31:5** If I have walked with vanity, or if my foot hath hasted to deceit; **31:6** Let me be weighed in an even balance that God may know mine integrity.

If we depart from God and from enthusiastically learning, internalizing and living by every Word of God; we are under a curse for our spiritual adultery and idolatry, as well as the specific sins involved.

31:7 If my step hath turned out of the way, and mine heart walked after mine [the lust of the] eyes, and if any blot hath cleaved to mine hands; **31:8** Then let me sow, and let another eat; yea, let my offspring be rooted out.

31:9 If mine heart have been deceived by a woman [spiritually a false teacher, false doctrine], or if I have laid wait at my neighbour's door; **31:10** Then let my wife grind [serve] unto another, and let others bow down [lie] upon her.

Adultery is a great sin; and the spiritual adultery of departing from Jesus Christ and from living by every Word of God, to follow and obey strange teachings of a strange god IS spiritual adultery.

31:11 For this is an heinous crime; yea, it is an iniquity to be punished by the judges. **31:12** For it is a fire that consumeth to destruction, and would root out all mine increase.

If we are not just with others God will not hold us guiltless: all persons are equal before him.

31:13 If I did despise the cause of my manservant or of my maidservant, when they contended with me; **31:14** What then shall I do when God riseth up? and when he visiteth, what shall I answer him? **31:15** Did not he that made me in the womb make him? and did not one fashion us in the womb?

31:16 If I have withheld the poor from their desire, or have caused the eyes of the widow to fail; **31:17** Or have eaten my morsel myself alone, and the fatherless hath not eaten thereof; **31:18** (For from my youth he was brought [my neighbor] up with me, as with a father, and I have guided her from my mother's womb;)

If the wealthy or the better off, do not help the needy; it is a great evil. And if the spiritually blessed do not feed the poor in spirit, with the solid meat of God's Word; it is a great sin.

Elders must give an account for the spiritual health of God's flocks entrusted to their care. If they are lacking in spiritual growth, the shepherds will be judged for that.

31:19 If I have seen any perish for want of clothing, or any poor without covering; **31:20** If his loins have not blessed me, and if he were not warmed with the fleece of my sheep; **31:21** If I have lifted up my hand against the fatherless, when I saw my help in the gate: **31:22** Then let mine arm fall from my shoulder blade, and mine arm be broken from the bone.

Fear God and feed his sheep with the Word of God! Do not be like the Laodicean shepherds of Ezekiel 34 who feed themselves and not the sheep; or who feed the sheep only enough to keep them almost alive, and give them polluted spiritual food and water in place of the pure Word of God.

31:23 For destruction from God was a terror to me, and by reason of his highness I could not endure.

Never trust in transitory physical riches in place of the riches of the spirit and eternal life!

Never say "I am righteous, for I am rich in money and followers"! For that is spiritual idolatry!

Compromising with God's Word to gain more followers and income, is spiritual adultery; it is lusting after such things instead of obedience to our espoused Husband!

31:24 If I have made gold my hope, or have said to the fine gold, Thou art my confidence; **31:25** If I rejoice because my wealth was great, and because mine hand had gotten much;

To read horoscopes and trust in the heavenly bodies or to trust in the false traditions of men which are contrary to the Word of God, is also spiritual adultery and idolatry. To believe such false gods and false doctrines is to deny the Eternal!

31:26 If I beheld the sun when it shined, or the moon walking in brightness; **31:27** And my heart hath been secretly enticed, or my mouth hath kissed my hand: **31:28 This also were an iniquity to be punished by the judge: for I should have denied the God that is above.**

It is a sin to curse even the wicked; we are to pray for them, that they will sincerely repent and overcome the evil.

31:29 If I rejoice at the destruction of him that hated me, or lifted up myself when evil found him: **31:30** Neither have I suffered my mouth to sin by wishing a curse to his soul.

No man could say that Job did not care for them. Job satisfied them all and no man could say otherwise.

31:31 If the men of my tabernacle [tent, household, life] said not, Oh that we had of his flesh! we cannot be satisfied.

Job had fed the needy and housed the stranger

31:32 The stranger did not lodge in the street: but I opened my doors to the traveller.

Job did not try to hide any transgression like Adam tried to hide his sin.

31:33 If I covered my transgressions as Adam, by hiding mine iniquity in my bosom:

Job feared God and did not fear what men can do.

31:34 Did I fear a great multitude, or did the contempt of families terrify me, that I kept silence, and went not out of the door? **31:35** Oh that one would hear me! behold, my desire is, that the Almighty would answer me, and **that mine adversary had written a book**. **31:36** Surely I would take it [the adversary's book of accusations] upon my shoulder, and bind it as a crown to me. **31:37** I would declare unto him [the accusing adversary] the number of my steps; as a prince would I go near unto him.

31:38 If my land cry against me, or that the furrows likewise thereof complain; **31:39** If I have eaten the fruits thereof without money [by stealing], or have caused the owners thereof to lose their life: **31:40** Let thistles grow instead of wheat, and cockle instead of barley [in my own fields].

The words of Job are ended.

The book of Job now gets to the root and foundation of Job's problem, which is exactly the same as the problem in today's assemblies: Laodicean lukewarmness produced by: **SELF-JUSTIFICATION**.

Up to this point Job's three friends had been falsely accusing Job of sin without presenting any specific proofs, and Job had been responding by justifying himself.

Job had indeed not sinned, yet he had been self-justifying over his condition; and his belief that a righteous God could not afflict the righteous made Job's self-justifying complaints come very close to accusing God of wrongful conduct in afflicting him.

Until now I have tried to avoid any mention of Job as being self-righteous, because many people simply say that Job was self-righteous, close the book, and avoid the many other instructional details of the book.

I wanted to focus on the many other aspects of Job because the book is not about self-righteousness only. This is because Job is NOT a one subject book.

During the course of the discussion between Job and his friends, very many important points are been covered about the power and glory of God;

the end of the wicked; the various duties of man and various sins; and the questions of why the innocent suffer in this life.

These four men had not understood the issue, which is that the Creator can do what he wants with his creation and that we are all possessions of our Creator, and that our Creator does as he pleases for the purpose of perfecting his creation.

Jesus Christ was perfect and yet he learned through the things that he suffered. One of the most important lessons learned was how to empathize and understand the sufferings of the people under Satan's yoke, so that Christ could be the best possible Intercessor between man and God.

Even so, those who are called out of sin to become part of the priest-hood of our High Priest, Jesus Christ must also be TESTED and afflicted for the same reasons.

Job's friends wrongfully accused him of sin because Job was afflicted; and Job not understanding what was happening, came very close to accusing God of wrongdoing, by justifying himself against the instructive affliction of God.

Brethren, very, very, soon now, most of today's called out will be in great tribulation and only a few faithfully zealous will be spared for another kind of trial.

Perhaps the greatest lesson of Job is that physical riches are deceitful, and that compared to God; there is NOT ONE RIGHTEOUS. We can only try to put on the righteousness of God through learning, internalizing and living by every Word of God, being totally faithful to God the Father and to our espoused Husband, Jesus Christ; no matter what our circumstances, good or bad.

> **Hebrews 5:8** Though he were a Son, yet learned he obedience by the things which he suffered;

> **Hebrews 2:17** Wherefore in all things it behoved him to be made like unto his brethren, that he might be a merciful and faithful high priest in things pertaining to God, to make reconciliation for the sins of the people. **2:18 For in that he himself hath suffered being tempted, he is able to succour them that are tempted.**

Job 32

Elihu Speaks

Job 32:1 So these three men ceased to answer Job, **because he was righteous in his own eyes. 32:2** Then was kindled the wrath of Elihu the son of Barachel the Buzite, of the kindred of Ram: against Job was his wrath kindled, **because he justified himself rather than God.**

32:3 Also against his three friends was his wrath kindled, because they had found no answer, and yet had condemned Job [without cause].

Elihu had sat back and listened to the arguments before coming forward with his own comments.

32:4 Now Elihu had waited till Job had spoken, because they were elder than he. **32:5** When Elihu saw that there was no [correct] answer in the mouth of these three men, then his wrath was kindled. **32:6** And Elihu the son of Barachel the Buzite answered and said, I am young, and ye are very old; wherefore I was afraid, and durst not shew you mine opinion.

A good understanding of spiritual things is a gift of God and is given to whoever God decides to give it to; godly wisdom in not exclusive to the aged, or to the mighty of the world.

32:7 I said, Days should speak, and multitude of years should teach wisdom. **32:8** But there is **a spirit in man: and the inspiration of the Almighty giveth them understanding. 32:9** Great men are not always wise: neither do the aged [always have good judgment] understand judgment.

Elihu then gives his own opinion: he days that the truth was hidden from them all, lest they should think that wisdom was from man and not a gift from God or that they might think that they had figured this out for themselves.

32:10 Therefore I said, Hearken to me; I also will shew mine opinion. **32:11** Behold, I waited for your words; I gave ear to your reasons, whilst ye searched out what to say. **32:12** Yea, I attended unto you, and, behold, there was none of you that convinced Job, or that answered his words: **32:13** Lest ye should say, We have found out wisdom: God thrusteth him down, not man.

Elihu would not speak like the other three

32:14 Now he hath not directed his words against me: neither will I answer him with your speeches.

Thereupon the men were quiet and listened to Elihu

32:15 They were amazed, they answered no more: they left off speaking. **32:16** When I had waited, (for [for them to hear Elihu] they spake not, but stood still, and answered no more;) **32:17** I said, I will answer also my part, I also will shew mine opinion.

Elihu is bursting with the wisdom of God at the ignorance of these four men.

32:18 For I am full of matter, the spirit within me constraineth me. **32:19** Behold, my belly is as wine which hath no vent; it is ready to burst like new bottles.

Elihu refuses to flatter these four great men and insists on speaking the truth. How rare and precious a thing are the true words of the wise, spoken with courage.

> **Proverbs 27:5** Open rebuke is better than secret love. **27:6** Faithful are the wounds of a friend; but the kisses of an enemy are deceitful.

These four were more righteous than today's Ekklesia, which clings to false traditions and rejects knowledge in order to idolize man and organizations.

32:20 I will speak, that I may be refreshed: I will open my lips and answer. **32:21 Let me not, I pray you, accept any man's person, neither let me give flattering titles unto man. 32:22 For I know not to give flattering titles; in so doing my maker would soon take me away.**

Job 33

Elihu addresses his comments to Job

Job 33:1 Wherefore, Job, I pray thee, hear my speeches, and hearken to all my words. **33:2** Behold, now I have opened my mouth, my tongue hath spoken in my mouth. **33:3** My words shall be of the uprightness of my heart: and my lips shall utter knowledge clearly.

Elihu says, "instead of ridiculing or rejecting my words; give me an answer if you can".

33:4 The spirit of God hath made me, and the breath of the Almighty hath given me life. **33:5** If thou canst answer me, set thy words in order before me, stand up.

Elihu stands in God's place to speak with Job as a kind of intercessor who is made of flesh. A man who prepares the way for Job to face God.

33:6 Behold, I am according to thy wish in God's stead: I also am formed out of the clay. **33:7** Behold, my terror shall not make thee afraid, neither shall my hand be heavy upon thee.

Elihu rehearses some of Job's own words

33:8 Surely thou hast spoken in mine hearing, and I have heard **the voice of thy words, saying**, **33:9** I am clean without transgression, I am innocent; neither is there iniquity in me. **33:10** Behold, he [God] findeth occasions against me, he counteth me for his enemy, **33:11** He putteth my feet in the stocks, he marketh all my paths.

Elihu hits the point square in his response. Who is Job (or any man) to demand an account of God)?

33:12 Behold, in this thou art not just: I will answer thee, **that God is greater than man. 33:13 Why dost thou strive against him? for he giveth not account of any of his matters.**

Though God speaks, yet it is not in man to understand [without repentance and the Spirit of understanding from God]

33:14 For God speaketh once, yea twice, yet man perceiveth it not. **33:15** In a dream, in a vision of the night, when deep sleep falleth upon men, in slumberings upon the bed; **33:16** Then he openeth the ears of men, and sealeth [directs their ways] their instruction, **33:17** That he may [convert man from sin] withdraw man from his purpose, and hide pride from man.

God gives life and saves man from destruction

33:18 He keepeth back his soul from the pit, and his life from perishing by the sword.

God afflicts whom he wills for his own purposes, which may include instruction and the perfecting of his people, as well as correction for sin.

33:19 He is chastened also with pain upon his bed, and the multitude of his bones with strong pain: **33:20** So that his life abhorreth bread, and his soul dainty meat. **33:21** His flesh is consumed away, that it cannot be seen; and his bones that were not seen stick out. **33:22** Yea, his soul draweth near unto the grave, and his life to the destroyers.

God sends his servants to teach the gospel of warning and repentance in the hope that men might be saved.

33:23 If there be a messenger with him [God], an interpreter, one among a thousand, to shew unto man his [God's] uprightness: **33:24** Then he [God is merciful to the repentant] is gracious unto him, and saith, Deliver him from going down to the pit [grave]: I [God] have found a ransom.

The repentant who have learned from their correction, will ultimately be raised up to life eternal.

33:25 His [the repentant] flesh shall be fresher [he shall be forgiven and made purer and more innocent than a child] than a child's: he shall return to the days of his youth: **33:26** He shall pray unto God, and he [God] will be favourable unto him: and he shall see his face with joy: for he will render unto man his righteousness.

The repentant will be delivered from the grave into eternal life

33:27 He looketh upon men, and if any say, I have sinned, and perverted that which was right, and it profited me not; **33:28** He will deliver his soul from going into the pit [grave], and his life shall see the light.

33:29 Lo, all these things worketh God oftentimes with man, **33:30** To bring back his soul from the pit [grave], to be enlightened with the light of the living.

Elihu speaks on and dares to say that he will teach wisdom to Job

33:31 Mark well, O Job, hearken unto me: hold thy peace, and I will speak. **33:32** If thou hast anything to say, answer me: speak, for I desire to justify thee. **33:33** If not, hearken unto me: hold thy peace, and I shall teach thee wisdom.

Job 34

Job 34:1 Furthermore Elihu answered and said, **34:2** Hear my words, O ye wise men; and give ear unto me, ye that have knowledge. **34:3** For the ear [should well consider] trieth words, as the mouth tasteth meat.

34:4 Let us choose to us [godly] judgment: let us know among ourselves what is good. **34:5** For Job hath said, I am righteous: and God hath taken away my [just] judgment.

34:6 Should I lie against my [what is right] right? my wound is incurable without [with unrepentant] transgression.

Elihu declares Job to be a righteous man who remains righteous even in the company of the wicked.

34:7 What man is like Job, who drinketh up scorning like water? **34:8** Which goeth in company with the workers of iniquity, and walketh with wicked men.

Job listened to the words of his friends debating with them; and they do not listen to the Word of God. Job, by justifying himself and not seeking out the advantage in God's correction; came to the conclusion that while he will obey God, there is no profit in such obedience.

34:9 For he [Job] hath said, It profiteth a man nothing that he should delight himself with God.

Elihu justifies GOD! While Job justified himself!

34:10 Therefore hearken unto me ye men of understanding: far be it from God, that he should do wickedness; and from the Almighty, that he should commit iniquity. **34:11** For the work of a man shall he render unto him, and cause every man to find according to his ways. **34:12** Yea, surely God will not do wickedly, neither will the Almighty pervert judgment.

God is Creator and has power over all flesh, to do whatever God wills

34:13 Who hath given him a charge over the earth? or who hath disposed the whole world? **34:14** If he set his heart upon man, if he gather unto himself his spirit and his breath; **34:15** All flesh shall perish together, and man shall turn again unto dust.

How could God be Creator and Ruler if he was not just?

34:16 If now thou hast understanding, hear this: hearken to the voice of my words.

34:17 Shall even he that hateth [justice and the right] right govern? and wilt thou condemn him [God] that is [the most] most just? **34:18** Is it fit to say to a king, Thou art wicked? and to princes, Ye are ungodly? **34:19** How much less to him that accepteth not the persons of princes, nor regardeth the rich more than the poor? for they all are the work of his hands.

If God judged people as we deserve; we would all perish

34:20 In a moment shall they [the wicked] die, and the people shall be troubled at midnight, and pass away: and the mighty shall be taken away without hand. **34:21** For his eyes are upon the ways of man, and he seeth all his goings.

Nothing can be hidden from God

34:22 There is no darkness, nor shadow of death, where the workers of iniquity may hide themselves.

God will not judge and condemn unequally; for then men could argue that God is unfair

34:23 For he will not lay upon man more than right; that he should enter into judgment with God. **34:24** He shall break in pieces [unrepentant both great and low] mighty men without number, and set others in their stead. **34:25** Therefore he knoweth their works, and he overturneth them [wickedness] in the night, so that they are destroyed.

Hear you churches; Those who begin to tolerate sin and compromise with God's Word will be afflicted by God; because they have no zeal for righteousness.

34:26 He striketh them as wicked men in the open sight of others; **34:27** Because they turned back from him, and would not consider any of his ways: **34:28** So that they cause the cry of the poor to come unto him, and he heareth the cry of the afflicted.

God is mighty; who can change his will?

34:29 When he giveth quietness, who then can make trouble? and when he hideth his face, who then can behold him? whether it be done against a nation, or against a man only: **34:30** That the hypocrite reign not, lest the people be ensnared.

It is good to repent before God

34:31 Surely it is meet to be said unto God, I have borne chastisement, I will not offend any more: **34:32** That which I see not teach thou me: if I have done iniquity, I will do no more.

34:33 Should it be according to thy mind? he will recompense it, whether thou refuse, or whether thou choose; and not I: therefore speak what thou knowest.

34:34 Let men of understanding tell me, and let a wise man hearken unto me.

34:35 Job hath spoken without knowledge, and his words were without wisdom. **34:36** My desire is that Job may be tried unto the end [his repentance] because of his answers for wicked men.

34:37 For he addeth rebellion unto his sin, he clappeth his hands among us, and multiplieth his words against God.

These are very profound words. Job had not sinned before this trial and TEST; and during his affliction he had refused to sin against God for his trials.

What then was Job's sin?

SELF-JUSTIFICATION!

Job continually justified himself instead of acknowledging that God has the right to perfect his creation in the manner that God deems best.

By justifying himself, Job was implying that God was unjust.

When we are afflicted, we are to go to God and say:

"Thank you Father for this trial. Please show me if I have done wrong, and reveal to me the lesson that I need to learn. HELP me to learn from this experience and to stop doing any sin, and HELP me to be a better person in future because of the experience. Make this trial a learning and growing experience for me, and help me to become more like you."

Job's sin was personal pride and an insistence that he was sinless and perfect before God; therefore while he did not directly attack God; he WAS blaming God in a round about way.

Job was rebellious in that he was resisting correction, and thereby accusing God of injustice!

> **Hebrews 12:5** And ye have forgotten the exhortation which speaketh unto you as unto children, My son, despise not thou the chastening of the Lord, nor faint when thou art rebuked of him:
>
> **12:6** For whom the Lord loveth he chasteneth, and scourgeth every son whom he receiveth. **12:7** If ye endure chastening, God dealeth with you as with sons; for what son is he whom the father chasteneth not?
>
> **12:8** But if ye be without chastisement, whereof all are partakers, then are ye bastards, and not sons.
>
> **12:9** Furthermore we have had fathers of our flesh which corrected us, and we gave them reverence: **shall we not much rather be in subjection unto the Father of spirits, and live?**

Why does God chastise his children? So that we might learn to be like HIM!

> **12:10** For they [our parents] verily for a few days chastened us after their own pleasure; but he [God] for our profit, **that we might be partakers of his holiness.**
>
> **12:11** Now no chastening for the present seemeth to be joyous, but grievous: nevertheless afterward it yieldeth the peaceable fruit of righteousness unto them which are exercised thereby.
>
> **12:12** Wherefore lift up the hands which hang down [in the affliction of correction], and the feeble knees [by repentance]; **12:13** And make straight [understand God's ways to walk in] paths for your feet, lest that which is lame [spiritually deficient] be turned out [go astray from God's Word] of the way; but let it rather be healed [by bowing to God's correcting and being spiritually healed].

God is a loving Father who corrects us according to his will for the purpose of bringing us to his righteousness.

This lesson on the evil of self-justification before God, is a very profound lesson for today's Spiritual Ekklesia. Self-Justification is the sin of Laodicea, who are zealous for their own idea of what is right, instead of for what Almighty God says is right! Who think they know it all and that they are justified in all that they do (Rev 3:16).

Self-justification comes out of pride and is the foundation of [sin] rebellion against God.

Today's leaders know the scriptures, yet they justify themselves by saying that their organization allows or teaches this or that and they will not accept the authority of God's Word above the human leadership. They utterly reject knowledge and understanding from God justifying that rejection by clinging to the false traditions of men.

God has this to say to the shepherds of this generation:

> **Hosea 4:6** My people are destroyed for lack of knowledge: **because thou hast rejected knowledge, I will also reject thee, that thou shalt be no priest to me: seeing thou hast forgotten the law of thy God**, I will also forget thy children. **4:7** As they were increased, so they sinned against me: therefore will I change their glory into shame.

They claim to be godly like Job; and they justify themselves like Job. Instead of going to the Word of God; they go to some man, human tradition or organization to justify themselves.

They self-justify and they reject the Word of God [even whole sections of Books like Nehemiah], which is the foundation of knowledge, for their own false traditions.

Job DID obey God; but his self-justification in the face of God's correction proved that he was more about what HE THOUGHT was right, than about what God commanded.

Today's church groups DO go through the motions of paying lip-service to and making a pretense of obeying God; but our self-justification in the face of God's Word proves that we are more about what WE THINK is right, than about what God commands.

There are even those who dare to declare "We do not keep the commandments because we must, we keep them because we want to." Such an attitude makes them the sovereign deciders and God subject to their whims.

God revealed this problem to Job through this trial; not to abuse Job, but to save him! For this self- justifying attitude will always lead to sin, because we will do what we think is right; instead of living by every Word of God (Mat 4:4).

Brethren, this state of self-justifying against God by justifying what WE THINK is right, instead of faithful, zealous obedience and submission to God; will lead to our correction, just like the correction of Job!

This is EXACTLY the state of today's major COG Groups and most of the brethren who do whatever the organization teaches; and "the church" does what they think is right by their false traditions and they do NOT live by every Word of God!

I tell you the truth: Our own tribulation is waiting at the door, and we shall all suffer as Job did unless we sincerely repent and turn to a genuine zeal to live by every Word of God

Job's trials are analogous of the soon coming great tribulation, when those in the faith who have the same problem of being just in their own eyes will be corrected as was Job.

Job 35

Job 35:1 Elihu spake moreover, and said, **35:2** Thinkest thou this to be right, that thou saidst, **My righteousness is more than God's? 35:3 For thou saidst, What advantage will it be unto thee? and, What profit shall I have, if I [repent and be cleansed] be cleansed from my sin? 35:4** I will answer thee, and thy companions with thee.

If we sin do we damage God? If we are righteous does that give anything to God? Who are we to think that we can teach God anything? It is HE who teaches US; Not we who teach HIM!

35:5 Look unto the heavens, and see; and behold the clouds which are higher than thou.

35:6 If thou sinnest, what doest thou against him? or if thy transgressions be multiplied, what doest thou unto him? **35:7** If thou be righteous, what givest thou him? or what receiveth he of thine hand?

Our good or evil only affects ourselves and other humans

35:8 Thy wickedness may hurt a man as thou art; and thy righteousness may profit the son of man. **35:9** By reason of the multitude of oppressions they make the oppressed to cry: they cry out by reason of the arm of the mighty.

Wicked men do not acknowledge God and his Word

35:10 But none [of the unrepentant wicked] saith, Where is God my maker, who giveth songs in the night; **35:11** Who teacheth us more than the beasts of the earth, and maketh us wiser than the fowls of heaven? **35:12** There they cry, but none giveth answer, because of the pride of evil men.

Trust in God for he judges all men and he has no patience with self-justification.

35:13 Surely God will not hear vanity, neither will the Almighty regard it. **35:14** Although thou sayest thou shalt not see him, yet judgment is before him; therefore trust thou in him.

Job trusted in his wealth as an indication of his own righteousness and did not truly trust in God who gives and takes away these physical things. Sound familiar? Today's called out put their trust in numbers and income as a [false] measure of their righteousness; therefore God will take away the riches in which we trust to turn us back to him!

35:15 But now, because it is not so, he hath visited in his anger; yet he [Job and friends do not understand] knoweth it not in great extremity: **35:16** Therefore doth Job open his mouth in vain; he multiplieth words without knowledge.

Job 36

Job 36:1 Elihu also proceeded, and said, **36:2** Suffer [be patient and permit me to speak] me a little, and I will shew thee that I have yet to speak on God's behalf. **36:3** I will fetch my knowledge from afar [from God's inspiration], and will ascribe righteousness to my Maker.

36:4 For truly my words shall not be false: he that is perfect in knowledge [God] is with thee [teaching Job through affliction].

God is fair and just

36:5 Behold, God is mighty, and despiseth not any: he is mighty in strength and wisdom. **36:6** He preserveth not the life of the wicked: but giveth right to the poor.

The righteous who learn and live by every Word of God will be resurrected and set as kings on their thrones.

36:7 He withdraweth not his eyes from the righteous: but with kings are they on the throne; yea, he doth **establish them for ever, and they are** [will be] **exalted**.

If the righteous are afflicted it is for their own good, to perfect them and train them for future glory

36:8 And if they be bound in fetters, and be holden in cords of affliction; **36:9** Then he sheweth them their work, and their transgressions that they have exceeded. **36:10** He openeth also their ear to discipline, and commandeth that they return from iniquity.

36:11 If they **obey and serve him**, they shall [in eternity] spend their days in prosperity, and their years in pleasures [for the things of God are a pleasure to the faithful]. **36:12 But if they obey not, they shall perish by the sword, and they shall die without knowledge.**

Those who tolerate false doctrine and sin for the sake of organizational "unity" will be sternly corrected along with all those who compromise with or break any part of the Word of God.

The hypocrites who place burdens on others that they will not bear themselves, and who sin or do not practice what they teach, will be destroyed.

36:13 But the hypocrites in heart heap up wrath : they cry not when he bindeth them. [upon themselves] **36:14** They die in youth, and their life is among the unclean.

God delivers the poor in spirit and feeds them; opening his ears to their cries

36:15 He delivereth the poor in his affliction, and openeth their ears in oppression.

God would have delivered Job, except that Job fell into wickedness through justifying himself against God

36:16 Even so would he have removed thee out of the strait into a broad place, where there is no straitness; and that which should be set on thy table should be full of fatness. **36:17** But thou hast fulfilled the judgment of the wicked: judgment and justice take hold on thee.

The Unpardonable Sin

Job is warned that he is about to be destroyed by God for justifying himself against God; just like today's Spiritual Ekklesia is facing destruction for justifying themselves against God and his Word in order to remain faithful to their idols of men, false traditions and organizations.

Job was an otherwise righteous man, but today's called out Spiritual Ekklesia is full of sin and in very grave danger of the unpardonable sin! Which unpardonable sin IS self-justification against God and a refusal to repent!

If we refuse to repent, justifying ourselves against God; there is no more sacrifice for our sins (Heb 10:26)!

The great tribulation correction is all that remains to SAVE the various organizations of today's Spiritual Ekklesia from damnation, for our self-justification and refusal to repent and our rejection of zeal for God's Word for OUR OWN false traditions, organizations and men!

It is not for nothing that Jesus Christ WARNED US that he will spew us out of his body!

> **Revelation 3:16** So then because thou art lukewarm, and neither cold nor hot, I will **spue** thee out of my mouth.
>
> **Hebrews 10:26** For if we sin wilfully after that we have received the knowledge of the truth, there remaineth no more sacrifice for sins,

Brethren, Jesus Christ was getting angry with Job's self-justification, and God IS ANGRY with today's Assemblies and brethren for the same sin [even though we are far more sinful than Job]! Self-justification brings a REFUSAL to REPENT because we are just in our own eyes!

Self-justification is the great sin that required God's correction to save Job spiritually, and it is the great sin which requires God's correction for the various organizations of today's Ekklesia who will be rejected by God the Father and Jesus Christ and corrected in the affliction of great tribulation in the hope that we might, like Job; be saved.

Job 36:18 Because there is wrath, beware lest he take thee away with his stroke: then a great ransom cannot deliver thee.

Will Christ esteem us when we justify ourselves against God the Father, against the Word of God and against HIM? Quickly repent and turn to live by every Word of God, because NOTHING can deliver us from the wrath of God.

36:19 Will he esteem thy riches? no, not gold, nor all the forces of strength. **36:20** Desire not the night [do not seek our own affliction by justifying ourselves against God], when people are cut off in their place.

Choose repentance and humility before God and his Word, and flee from all self-justification and iniquity.

36:21 Take heed, regard not iniquity: for this hast thou chosen rather than affliction.

Remember that God is our Teacher; What is man that he presumes to know better than the Word of God? STOP calling the Sabbath Holy and then routinely polluting it!

Stop exalting loyalty to men, false traditions, or organization, as if being loyal to them was loyalty to God! Stop committing spiritual adultery with our own little tin gods; exalting them above the Word of the Almighty!

STOP exalting ourselves and not exalting our Mighty Savior to live by every Word of God!

36:22 Behold, God exalteth by his power: who teacheth like him? **36:23** Who hath enjoined him his way? or who can say, Thou hast wrought iniquity? **36:24** Remember that thou [should] magnify his work, which men behold. **36:25** Every man may see it; man may behold it afar off.

God is great, He is Mighty, He is Wise! Who is man to justify himself before his Maker?

36:26 Behold, God is great, and we know him not, neither can the number of his years be searched out.

See how these things of nature were understood thousands of years ago? Ancient man was NOT ignorant man!

36:27 For he maketh small the drops of water: they pour down rain according to the vapour thereof: **36:28** Which the clouds do drop and distil upon man abundantly.

36:29 Also can any understand the spreadings of the clouds, or the noise [the thunder] of his tabernacle [clouds]? **36:30** Behold, he spreadeth his light upon it, and covereth the bottom of the sea.

By the rain from God the people are fed with the produce of the earth.

36:31 For by them judgeth he the people; he giveth meat in abundance.

36:32 With clouds he covereth [can hide the light] the light; and commandeth it not to shine by the cloud that cometh betwixt. **36:33** The noise [thunder comes of the clouds] thereof sheweth concerning it, the cattle also [are fed by the watering of the grass] concerning the vapour.

Job 37

The Might and Wisdom of GOD!

NEVER justify ourselves; tremble before God and his Word: HEAR HIM and KEEP His wise Word!

Job 37:1 At this also my heart trembleth, and is moved out of his place. **37:2** Hear attentively the noise of his voice, and the sound that goeth out of his mouth. **37:3** He directeth it [His Word] under the whole heaven, and his lightning unto the ends of the earth.

From the cloud and the lightening God roars and thunders his voice; HEAR YE HIM!

37:4 After it a voice roareth: he thundereth with the voice of his excellency; and he will not stay [delay his words] them when his voice is heard.

The Might and Wisdom of GOD!

37:5 God thundereth marvellously with his voice; great things doeth he, which we cannot comprehend.

37:6 For he saith to the snow, Be thou on the earth; likewise to the small rain, and to the great rain of his strength. **37:7** He sealeth up the hand of every man [gives understanding of physical things]; that all men may know his work.

God has programmed the behavior of the brute beasts

37:8 Then the beasts go into dens, and remain in their places. **37:9** Out of the south cometh the whirlwind: and cold out of the north [in the northern hemisphere].

37:10 By the breath of God [moist wind in the cold] frost is given: and the breadth of the waters is straitened [contained].

God established the weather patterns

37:11 Also by watering he wearieth the thick cloud: he scattereth his bright cloud: **37:12** And it is turned round about by his counsels: that they may do whatsoever he commandeth them upon the face of the world in the earth.

God uses the weather, either for our correction or for a good blessing

37:13 He causeth it to come, whether for correction, or for his land, or for mercy.

Job is exhorted to listen to the wondrous works of God and to stop justifying himself against God. Today's church groups should also see these words and LISTEN and repent of justifying themselves against God: Lest they undergo the exact same correction Job did.

The latter day beloved of God who have become lukewarm and faithless will be cast into the furnace of great tribulation so that by afflicting the flesh the spirit might be saved.

What is our sin you ask? We reject godly knowledge to exalt our own ways and false traditions making the Word of God of no effect.

> **Matthew 15:7** Ye hypocrites, well did Esaias prophesy of you, saying, **15:8** This people draweth nigh unto me with their mouth, and honoureth me with their lips; but their heart is far from me. **15:9** But in vain they do worship me, teaching for doctrines the commandments of men.

Brethren, besides being a book of great wisdom and instruction: what happened to Job is an allegory of today's Ekklesia. We have a certain appearance and we pay lip service to godliness; but we justify ourselves and our own self-righteousness: and justifying ourselves, we refuse to sincerely repent and give up our own false ways to live by every Word of God the Almighty!

Like Job we will be afflicted until we learn to stop justifying ourselves and we sincerely repent of our own ways to embrace and live by EVERY WORD of ALMIGHTY GOD!

Oh, how God truly loves his people, his obstinate children; who think they know better than him! Because he loves us so very much, we are set for a good spanking to save us from ourselves.

>**Revelation 3: 19** As many as I love, I rebuke and chasten: be zealous therefore, and repent.

Understand the greatness and wisdom of God and sincerely repent of justifying ourselves against God!

Job 37:14 Hearken unto this, O Job: stand still, and consider the wondrous works of God.

37:15 Dost thou know when God disposed them, and caused the light of his cloud to shine? **37:16** Dost thou know the balancings of the clouds, the wondrous works of him which is perfect in knowledge? **37:17** How thy garments are warm, when he quieteth the earth by the south wind?

37:18 Hast thou with him spread out the sky, which is strong, and as a molten looking glass? **37:19** Teach us what we shall say unto him; for we cannot order our speech by reason of darkness [our ignorance compared to God's wisdom].

37:20 Shall it be told him [God] that I speak? if a man speak, surely he shall be swallowed up [man is nothing compared to the wisdom of God].

God's throne is in the heights of the North. The north wind is analogous of God's Word chasing away the clouds of spiritual darkness.

37:21 And now men see not the bright light which is in the clouds: but the wind passeth, and cleanseth them [chases the clouds away] . **37:22** Fair weather cometh out of the north [the north wind clearing the clouds]: with God is terrible majesty.

37:23 Touching the Almighty, we cannot find him out: he is excellent in power, and in judgment, and in plenty of justice: he will not afflict [unjustly].

37:24 [Righteous] Men do therefore fear him: he respecteth not any that are wise of [in their own minds, justifying themselves against God's wisdom] heart.

The Great Sin of Today's Spiritual Ekklesia

The conclusion of the book is a powerful lesson in humility and sincere repentance before God.

The Bering who later gave up his Godhood to be made flesh and die to redeem humanity as Jesus Christ explains to Job and to us the great sin of self-justification before God.

Why the Great Tribulation on Today's Spiritual Ekklesia

God spells out the situation in today's Spiritual Ekklesia.

Today's Spiritual Ekklesia has a certain love for God, but we have been led astray into thinking that following our own false traditions and idols of men rather than being diligent to live by every Word of God, somehow makes us right before God.

Therefore we justify ourselves and our own ways thinking that we are righteous before God in following men. This self-justification of our sins has separated us from God and made it almost impossible to repent because we genuinely believe ourselves to be righteous.

We have gone astray from zeal for the practical application of God's Word, and we justify ourselves claiming to be righteous and godly not realizing how wicked we really are in God's sight.

Today's Spiritual Ekklesia MUST; STOP equating loyalty to our false traditions, leaders and organizations with loyalty to God!

WE MUST STOP doing what we think is right; and WE MUST START exalting God and doing what GOD SAYS IS RIGHT IN HIS WORD.

If we truly loved God; we would be DOING what God says is right; NOT what we decide for ourselves is good and right!

Laodicea

To Laodicea Jesus identifies himself as the faithful and true witness of what they are truly like. They think themselves spiritually rich and have no idea what Jesus Christ really thinks of them. Jesus here tells them their problems straight out, but they are proud and wilfully blind to reality.

Laodicea means the people will be judged and corrected, For the definition and further details see:

Christ emphasizes that his message to Laodicea is true and is coming out of Christ's faithful love for them, in the hope that they might repent and be saved.

Jesus also calls himself the "beginning of the creation of God;" clearly meaning that Christ is the Creator who began the creation of all things. See Revelation 1:8. 1:11, 21:6, 22:13 I am the Alpha [Beginning]

Revelation 3:14 And unto the angel of the church of the Laodiceans write; These things saith the Amen, the faithful and true witness, the beginning of the creation of God;

Laodicea is spiritually lukewarm, professing godliness while keeping the commandments according to their own imaginations instead of keeping them the way that God commands.

They pay lip service to godliness without any zeal to learn and keep the Word of God. Their zeal is for their own ways and what they think, for their own past false traditions and their idols of men and not for what God says. They stand on their false past traditions and proudly think they know it all; refusing any spiritual growth they are stagnant or even falling backward in their spiritual condition.

They are hot for their own traditions, and for the teachings of their idols of men about the Word of God, and cold for zealously keeping the whole Word as God, as God has commanded them. This mixture of hot for their idols of men and corporate entities, and a cold, lack of zeal to keep the Word of God, makes them lukewarm and revolting to Christ.

They are idolaters of men and tradition; proud, thinking that they know it all spiritually and therefore refuse correction from God or man; they reject the Word of God for their own ways and they reject any growth in truth and refuse to turn from error.

This is a clear, obvious, indisputable and precise explanation of the overwhelming majority in the Ekklesia today!

Because these folks have rejected Christ to follow him above our idols of men they will be rejected by Christ into the correction of great tribulation, in the hope that through the correction of the flesh the spirit may be saved.

3:15 I know thy works, that thou art neither cold nor hot: I would thou wert cold or hot. **3:16** So then because thou art lukewarm, and neither cold nor hot, **I will spue thee out of my mouth** [They will be rejected by Christ into severe correction] .

Proud and self-willed, they think they are spiritually rich and know it all, having need of no spiritual growth, and they reject the increase in spiritual knowledge and understanding promised for the last days, Daniel 12.

They reject any part of scripture which they do not want to follow, saying it is for others; and they are so proud and arrogant they have no idea how spiritually wretched, miserable and poor they really are.

They are wilfully blind to their own condition and to the things of God that disprove their own false ways; They lack the garments of righteousness and are naked of any righteousness before God their many sins exposed to Him; beginning with the sins of pride and self- justification and self-approval.

3:17 Because thou sayest, I am rich [spiritually], and increased with goods [spiritual knowledge], and have need of nothing [no one not even Christ (the Word of God) can tell them anything]; and knowest not that thou art [spiritually] wretched, and miserable, and [spiritually] poor [knowing almost nothing of God as they ought to know it], and blind [willfully blind to their wretched spiritual state], and naked [naked of any true godly righteousness, not being zealous to keep the Word of God]:

Christ counsels those with the Laodicean attitude to buy spiritual gold in the fire of tribulation; that they may become spiritually rich.

They are bidden to sincerely repent of their prideful sins so that the nakedness of their wickedness may be covered by the application of the sacrifice of Christ; and so that they may receive God's Holy Spirit and the white raiment of the righteousness of the zealous keeping of the whole Word of God.

They are commanded to anoint their eyes and open them to see themselves as God sees them, and to sincerely repent from their pride and false ways and to turn away from their idols of men and false traditions to follow the spirit of God into all truth; rejecting all error and sin to embrace godly truth that they might be saved.

3:18 I counsel thee to buy of me [spiritual] gold tried in the fire [during the period of your correction in the fire of tribulation], that thou mayest be [become spiritually rich] rich; and white raiment [the righteousness of zealously keeping the whole Word of God], that thou mayest be clothed, and that the shame of thy nakedness [that our sins might be covered by the righteousness of God] do not appear; and anoint thine eyes with eyesalve, [acquire the Holy Spirit through sincere repentance] that thou mayest see [open our eyes to see ourselves as God sees us, to see ourselves as we really are, so that we can repent and be saved].

Jesus reminds these folks that he rebukes them only because he truly loves them and is not willing that they should perish. They are rejected only because they first rejected Christ, refusing to keep the whole Word of God, refusing to follow Christ and refusing to live by every Word of God in Christ-like zeal.

Jesus Christ tells those of the Laodicean attitude; which is the overwhelming attitude throughout the Ekklesia today; to REPENT of their pride and self-righteousness; and to REPENT of trusting in their idols of men and false traditions.

Jesus Christ tells us to turn to him; and turn to a zeal for the whole Word of God, to learn it and to keep it; to turn from our false idols and false traditions and to become zealous to remove error and embrace the truth of God!

3:19 As many as I love, I rebuke and chasten: be zealous therefore, and repent.

Jesus is warning and calling each one of his straying sheep; He wants them to open up to him, to reject idols of men and false traditions and to follow him, to be zealous to remove sin and to embrace God's righteous truth, to internalize the solid meat of the Word of God in fellowship with Christ and God the Father.

They have an open invitation from Jesus Christ who is gladly willing to accept them, if they would only open up their eyes and turn to Him!

3:20 Behold, I stand at the door, and knock: if any man hear my voice, and open the door, I will come in to him, and will sup [eat; internalize the Word of God] with him, and he with me.

Only those who overcome this Laodicean attitude of pride and self-will will be resurrected to spirit. Those who sincerely repent of the sins of Laodicea will be in the resurrection to eternal life and will have a place in the eternal government of God.

3:21 To him that overcometh will I grant to sit with me in my throne, even as I also overcame, and am set down with my Father in his throne.

3:22 He that hath an ear, let him hear what the Spirit saith unto the churches.

As the seventh and last church addressed, Laodicea has all of the problems of the other churches.

That is because pride is the chief cause of most of the various problems. Today we are full of pride and idolatry, rejecting any biblical thing we do not agree with, claiming it applies only to others.

They think of themselves as the repository of all wisdom and truth, and refuse any zeal to keep the whole Word of God, in order to follow their corporate idols, idols of men and their own false traditions.

They call the Sabbath and High Days, Holy; and then walk all over them, while claiming that the commandments not to cook or buy food on Sabbath somehow apply to others and not to themselves. They insist on following the apostate Rabbinic Calendar and refuse to keep the Biblical Calendar of God; even though the proofs are now overwhelming.

They have almost no understanding of the Festivals, rejecting the true meanings of the Festivals; even still claiming that the seven day Feast of Tabernacles somehow represents only one thousand years. They reject any zeal for keeping the Word of God, and insist on a zeal for the corporate idols, idols of men and past false traditions, insisting that people should obey them, above the Word of God.

The Mosaic Pharisees were a type of Laodicea

The Laodicean attitude is an exact replica of the primary attitude of the Mosaic Pharisees during the physical ministry of Christ.

Contrary to popular belief the Mosaic Pharisees were NOT zealous for the law, rather they made the law of God of no effect by their own false traditions just as today's modern Ekklesia does!

In Matthew 15:9 Jesus said of the Mosaic Pharisees; and this is a very precise description of the Ekklesia today:

Matthew 15:7 Ye hypocrites, well did Esaias prophesy of you, saying, **15:8 This people draweth nigh unto me with their mouth, and honoureth me with their lips; but their heart is far from me. 15:9 But in vain they do worship me, teaching for doctrines the commandments of men.**

Matthew 23 describes the attitude during the physical ministry of Jesus Christ; and it also accurately describes the church of God groups right before Christ comes to rule: today!

Matthew 23:1 Then spake Jesus to the multitude, and to his disciples,

At that time the scribes and Pharisees sat in Moses seat; that changed with the death and resurrection of Christ who then became our High Priest forever.

We are to obey men when they speak the truth of God, and are NOT to obey them when they depart from the Word of God!

23:2 Saying The scribes and the Pharisees sit in Moses' seat: **23:3** All therefore whatsoever they bid you observe, that observe and do; but do not ye after their works: for they say, and do not.

Today's corporate churches also bind heavy burdens on the brethren, mainly financial.

23:4 For they bind heavy burdens and grievous to be borne, and lay them on men's shoulders; but they themselves will not move them with one of their fingers.

With the death of the Husband of Israel; the marriage between physical Mosaic Israel and Christ ended, and so did the authority of the Mosaic Priesthood and the Pharisees!

When Jesus Christ ascended into heaven and was accepted by God the Father as a sacrifice for us; He became our High Priest and the King of the world in waiting; the Mosaic priesthood was superseded by a reestablishment of the High Priesthood of Melchizedek.

From that time on; neither Levi, nor the Jews have any lawful spiritual authority, they have rejected the only lawful authority in existence at this time and forever more; which is the authority of our eternal High Priest Jesus Christ under God the Father.

The true and only existing Priesthood of God today is that of our High Priest Jesus Christ, and the called out have the potential to become priests of Christ forever in the coming Kingdom of God. All of us are in training to become priests forever in that spiritual priesthood of Jesus Christ [Melchizedek].

We are not to rely on apostate Christ rejecting, true priesthood rejecting persons for our religion! We are to rely on the example and teachings of our Lord Jesus Christ and the whole body of scriptures that were inspired by HIM!

Sadly, today many would be like those Pharisees; and many do indeed bind heavy burdens on the brethren that they would not lift a finger to bear themselves. This varies in intensity by each group as do all these other condemnations.

23:5 But all their works they do for to be seen of men: they make broad their phylacteries, and enlarge the borders of their garments, **23:6** And love the uppermost rooms at feasts, and the chief seats in the synagogues, **23:7** And greetings in the markets, and to be called of men, Rabbi, Rabbi.

Sound familiar? Just substitute the word "Mr". or "Pope" or "father" or "padre" etc for Rabbi!

Oh how we love titles and the chief seats today. Oh how many elders love to be greeted with fawning subservience and called by some title!

23:8 But be not ye called Rabbi [our religious master]: for one is your [religious master] Master, even Christ; and all ye [everyone in the Ekklesia are brothers including elders etc] are brethren. **23:9** And call no man your father [as a religious title] upon the earth: for one is your Father, which is in heaven. 23:10 Neither be ye called masters: for one is your Master, even Christ.

This is a condemnation of the love of position and titles!

It was always customary to call everyone brothers and sisters, including elders. Elders were introduced as elder ******, or brother ******; until Constantine and the Popes introduced layers of authority between the people and themselves; with the Pope between all others and God; with his pyramid system, that Christ says he hates.

This Babylonian Mystery Nicolaitane system has been introduced into the Ekklesia; which had until the 1930's called its elders "Brother "name."

God's government is NOT a pyramid.

God's governmental system is Family, with God the Father as the HEAD, and the firstborn son Jesus Christ as the second Head under God the Father, and then the Husbands over their own families.

Offices of ecclesiastical authority exist as helps to keep us focused on God the Father, Jesus Christ and the Word of God. Their authority comes from the Word of God and the truth that they teach, and once they depart from the Word of God they lose all moral authority!

1 Timothy 2:5 For there is one God, and one mediator between God and men, the man Christ Jesus; 2:6 Who gave himself a ransom for all, to be testified in due time.

The Nicolaitane idea of a pyramidal structure of layers of human authority between men and God is an abomination to God. It is the job of ALL elders to focus all people on the Father and Christ: NEVER to COME BETWEEN the people and God; but to act as facilitators in helping men to focus DIRECTLY on their Father through their ONLY High Priest and Mediator; Jesus Christ!

1 Corinthians 11:3 But I would have you know, that the head of every man is Christ; and the head of the woman is the man; and the head of Christ is God.

We are to prove the words of ALL men, by the Word of Almighty God! We are NOT to interpret God's Word by the words of men; but to prove the words of men by the Word of Almighty God!

Matthew 23:11 But he that is greatest among you shall be your servant.

We are all to desire to humbly and passionately serve our God and not to exalt ourselves. God will exalt or abase as HE sees fit.

23:12 And whosoever shall exalt himself shall be abased; and he that shall humble himself shall be exalted.

23:13 But woe unto you, scribes and Pharisees, hypocrites! for ye shut up the kingdom of heaven against men: for ye neither go in yourselves, neither suffer ye them that are entering to go in.

How? By paying lip-service to the law while making it of no effect by the traditions of men; and through compromise in its practical application; By making corporate idols and idols of men instead of faithfully putting God and His Word above all men, no matter what titles they claim.

23:14 Woe unto you, scribes and Pharisees, hypocrites! for ye devour widows' houses, and for a pretence make long prayer: therefore ye shall receive the greater damnation.

Demanding money from poor widows, and then making a show of flowery prayer.

23:15 Woe unto you, scribes and Pharisees, hypocrites! for ye compass sea and land to make one proselyte, and when he is made, ye make him twofold more the child of hell than yourselves.

How? By teaching them to obey men, organizations and false traditions, instead of focusing them on repentance and a diligent passionate obedience to all of God's words.

23:16 Woe unto you, ye blind guides, which say, Whosoever shall swear by the temple, it is nothing; but whosoever shall swear by the gold of the temple, he is a debtor! **23:17** Ye fools and blind: for whether is greater, the gold, or the temple that sanctifieth the gold? **23:18** And, Whosoever shall swear by the altar, it is nothing; but whosoever sweareth by the gift that is upon it, he is guilty. **23:19** Ye fools and blind: for whether is greater, the gift, or the altar that sanctifieth the gift? **23:20** Whoso therefore shall swear by the altar, sweareth by it, and by all things thereon.

Today's corporate Ekklesia exalts mammon and numbers; above repentance, faith and obedience to every Word of God.

23:21 And whoso shall swear by the temple, sweareth by it, and by him that dwelleth therein. **23:22** And he that shall swear by heaven, sweareth by the throne of God, and by him that sitteth thereon.

The important thing is NOT the numbers of responses, but the quality of the message!

The important thing is not the building [the organization] but serving and obeying the Eternal God on his throne, sitting in absolute authority over your deeds and very thoughts! and serving the God who shall most certainly judge us by our works; whether of faithful uncompromising obedience; or of compromising with HIS Word!

23:23 Woe unto you, scribes and Pharisees, hypocrites! for ye pay tithe of mint and anise and cummin, and have omitted the weightier matters of the law, judgment, mercy, and faith: these ought ye to have done, and not to leave the other undone.

Demanding every last cent that can be demanded or extorted, while ignoring and not rebuking sin, nor teaching repentance from evil doing, and expounding and exhorting faith, mercy and sound judgment founded on the basics of God's word and commandments.

We are to be merciful to the poor in their needs; we are to be merciful to the repentant instead of condemning them for being over righteous!

We are to preach a message of warning and repentance and the mercy of God [the Father] or the sincerely repentant; who gave his only begotten son that sinners might be reconciled to Him [the Father].

23:24 Ye blind guides, which strain at a gnat, and swallow a camel.

This is a figure of speech that simply means that we strain at the little unimportant things like money and numbers; and neglect the really important things like zeal for our God.

23:25 Woe unto you, scribes and Pharisees, hypocrites! for ye make clean the outside of the cup and of the platter, but within they are full of extortion and excess. **23:26** Thou blind Pharisee, cleanse first that which is within the cup and platter, that the outside of them may be clean also.

23:27 Woe unto you, scribes and Pharisees, hypocrites! for ye are like unto whited sepulchres, which indeed appear beautiful outward, but are within full of dead men's bones, and of all uncleanness. **23:28** Even so ye also outwardly appear righteous unto men, but within ye are full of hypocrisy and iniquity.

We have no business reaching out to the world with tainted messages, while we are full of sin inside ourselves and our organizations.

We need to clean up our own spiritual lives and get right with God. We need to rekindle our passionate zeal for God and his commandments; we need to get rid of those traditions not consistent with scripture; we need to start practicing what we preach, and to start setting a godly example instead of acting so shamefully.

We need to stop exalting men and organizations above God; we need to STOP equating loyalty to men, as being equal to loyalty to God. We need to repent and turn to our God with passionate enthusiastic consummate zeal; and then we need to begin to preach the Gospel of warning and repentance that Christ has commanded us to preach.

23:29 Woe unto you, scribes and Pharisees, hypocrites! because ye build the tombs of the prophets, and garnish the sepulchres of the righteous, **23:30** And say, If we had been in the days of our fathers, we would not have been partakers with them in the blood of the prophets.

We honour the prophets and ancient men of God, while persecuting those who are today filled with a similar zeal: Showing ourselves that we are no better than those who persecuted the saints of old.

23:31 Wherefore ye be witnesses unto yourselves, that ye are the children of them which killed the prophets. **23:32** Fill ye up then the measure of your fathers.

Today the corporate assemblies persecute the zealous for God just as the ancients persecuted the prophets and holy men, and as the Pharisees persecuted Christ and his true faithful disciples.

23:33 Ye serpents, ye generation of vipers, how can ye escape the damnation of hell? **23:34** Wherefore, behold, I send unto you prophets, and wise men, and scribes: and some of them ye shall kill and crucify; and some of them shall ye scourge in your synagogues, and persecute them from city to city: **23:35** That upon you may come all the righteous blood shed upon the earth, from the blood of righteous Abel unto the blood of Zacharias son of Barachias, whom ye slew between the temple and the altar.

Those who do such things are likened to vipers who hide along the path waiting to strike the unwary. When a person goes to them with questions, they reason with them that they should not be zealous like the Mighty Men of God, but should be lukewarm like themselves, then make a note to persecute such zeal by calling the zealous Pharisaical, when it is they themselves who are Pharisaic; filled with zeal for their own groups and traditions, while being lukewarm and compromising with the Word of God.

Since Cain slew Abel, it has ever been thus; that the faithless and compromised; have always persecuted the faithful and zealous. Those who exalt the Lord their God; will face resistance from outside and from inside these organizations,

Such Philadelphian pillars should REJOICE at the persecution from Laodicea, because they have been given an opportunity to set an example, that their persecutors will later remember and be convicted by.

These pillars persecuted by Laodicea should REJOICE, for they are being tempered and tested to become pillars in the Temple of The Great God for all eternity.

They that stand unshakable on the foundation of the Word of Almighty God; without turning, no matter what the stress; will be made fit by God to stand on that sure foundation of the Word of God as pillars, helping to hold up the entire family of God for all eternity!

23:36 Verily I say unto you, All these things shall come upon this generation.

These persecutions did come upon the saints by the religious establishment of that day, and have continued to this day. They are now being fulfilled internally by the Laodicean organizations.

23:37 O Jerusalem, Jerusalem, thou that killest the prophets, and stonest them which are sent unto thee, how often would I have gathered thy children together, even as a hen gathereth her chickens under her wings, and ye would not! **23:38** Behold, your house is left unto you desolate.

This is about the city, Jerusalem which persecuted the godly through history and is figuratively about the faithless who persecute the faithful today. Jesus Christ would have saved them, if only they would accept his deliverance and turn to him away from sin and compromise with the Father's law.

Both Jerusalem and today's faithless Ekklesia, will be made desolate in the tribulation; it is then that they will sincerely repent and turn to the ONLY one that can truly save!

23:39 For I say unto you, Ye shall not see me henceforth, till ye shall say, Blessed is he that cometh in the name of the Lord.

When you see Christ come, Jerusalem, and all those who persecuted the saints; will be in a humbled and repentant attitude, and will no longer reject Christ and the teachings of the whole Word of God; instead they shall Shout for Joy at his appearance; crying out "Blessed is he that cometh in the name of the Lord"!

Philadelphia and Laodicea

Jesus illustrated the difference between a Philadelphian and a Laodicean the difference between a holy attitude and a profane and unacceptable attitude in this parable.

These prayers are not just words, they reveal the attitude of the person praying, for out of the abundance of the heart the mouth speaks.

Luke 18:9 And he spake this parable unto certain which trusted in themselves that they were righteous, and despised others:

18:10 Two men went up into the temple to pray; the one a Pharisee [Laodicean], and the other a publican [Philadelphian].

18:11 The Pharisee [Laodicean] stood and prayed thus with himself, God, I thank thee, that I am not as other men are, extortioners, unjust, adulterers, or even as this publican.

18:12 I fast twice in the week, I give tithes of all that I possess.

18:13 And the publican [Sincerely repentant sinner; Philadelphian], standing afar off, would not lift up so much as his eyes unto heaven, but smote upon his breast, saying, God be merciful to me a sinner.

18:14 I tell you, this man went down to his house justified rather than the other: for every one that exalteth himself shall be abased; and he that humbleth himself shall be exalted.

Today the true Philadelphian pillars are scattered throughout the Ekklesia, which are overwhelmingly Laodicea.

Oh, how we Laodiceans exalt ourselves to live by our own false traditions and reject any true humble passion for our Mighty One who could deliver us! Proud and thinking ourselves rich in spiritual things, thinking we know it all: We have become spiritually dead, apostate from our Master.

Conclusion

The various church attitudes may have dominated at various historical tines, but the seven churches also each existed at the same time in the first century and each one is an instructional example for us, that all of these problems and strengths will also exist at the same time in these last days.

Today like Ephesus, we have lost the passionate zeal of our first love for truth and godliness and the whole Word of God.

Today like Smyrna, there are some who are faithful to God and God's Word and suffer much persecution.

Today like Pergamos, there are some who have not denied the authority of God and the scriptures and yet tolerate Nicolaitane bullying.

Today like Thyatira, there are those who are full of good works, but in their zeal to do good to their neighbor have lost sight of their obligations to God. Do NOT mistake love of man; for love of God!

As a bride is to be faithful to her husband, our first duty is to our spiritual Husband and all good works to others are secondary. Many unconverted people are also full of good works towards humanity and do not obey God;

how are we different from them if we are also full of good works for humanity and forget our LORD?

We should be filled with good works towards men; while not forgetting to put our LORD first in our lives!

What say you? If a bride put her personal charitable works ahead of her love and obedience to her husband, will the husband think that she loves her own works more than she loves him? It is a very good thing to do good works for people, but such good works should not overtake our zeal for our LORD!

Today, like Sardis, the overwhelming attitude in the Ekklesia is largely spiritually dead, having no fire of zeal to live by every Word of our LORD.

Today like Philadelphia, there are some faithful standing on the foundation of the whole Word of God; who are scattered like pillars throughout the various assemblies and standing alone. In a very short time now God's two servants will call for the faithful to gather together and leave for the place which God has prepared; the faithful pillars will respond to God's call while the others will not, thus separating out the faithful from the others.

Today like Laodicea, the Ekklesia is overwhelmingly proud, arrogant and unteachable by God. They reject large parts of God's Word and very much truth, to follow their idols of men and false traditions. They will not respond positively to God's warnings and the only way to save them from certain eternal death is to afflict the flesh to humble them so that the spirit might be saved.

Job 38

God Humbled Job and God will Humble Us

Job 38:1 Then the LORD answered Job out of the whirlwind [storm cloud], and said,

38:2 Who is this that darkeneth counsel by words without knowledge? **38:3** Gird up now thy loins like a man; for I will demand of thee, and answer thou me.

God demands of Job to answer if he was present at the creation as God was; and if Job knows how to create the earth? God mentions the angels as being there but not Job.

The same challenge is asked of today's Spiritual Ekklesia: Who are we to think that we can decide right from wrong for ourselves? Are we greater than God that we can bind and loose God's Word according to our own will?

38:4 Where wast thou when I laid the foundations of the earth? declare, if thou hast understanding. **38:5** Who hath laid the measures thereof, if thou knowest? or who hath stretched the line upon it? **38:6** Whereupon are the foundations thereof fastened? or who laid the corner stone thereof; **38:7**

When the morning stars [angels] sang together, and all the sons of God [angels] shouted for joy?

God asks Job if he knows that God separated the land from the sea on the first day. Implying the question: Could Job do that? The same question applies to us today; Could we do such things and if not who are we to question any part of God's Word or anything that God does?

38:8 Or who shut up the sea with doors [who caused the dry land to rise out of the sea], when it brake forth, as if it had issued out of the womb? **38:9** When I made the cloud the garment thereof, and thick darkness a swaddlingband for it, **38:10** And brake up for it my decreed place, and set bars and doors [set boundaries between the waters and the land], **38:11** And said, Hitherto shalt thou come, but no further: and here shall thy proud waves be stayed?

God asks Job if he has set the earth in rotation and created day and night; and set the limits of the lives of men? Brethren the very same question is before us: Did we do such things: If not who are we to justify ourselves before God the Almighty?

38:12 Hast thou commanded the morning since thy days; and caused the dayspring [dawn] to know his place; **38:13** That it might take hold of the ends of the earth, that the wicked might be shaken out of it? **38:14** It is turned [rotates] as clay to the seal; and they stand as a garment.

The light of life [eternal life] is withheld from the wicked and their strength will be broken.

38:15 And from the wicked their light is withholden, and the high arm shall be broken.

God asks: Does Job know what is under the sea? or does man know the secret of life and death? Can Job raise the dead? Brethren, can we make inanimate things live like god can?

38:16 Hast thou entered into the springs of the sea? or hast thou walked in the search of the depth? **38:17** Have the gates of death been opened unto thee? or hast thou seen the doors of the shadow of death? **38:18** Hast thou perceived the breadth of the earth? declare if thou knowest it all.

What is light and darkness? Did man make them? Have you lived from the beginning of all things?

38:19 Where is the way where light dwelleth? and as for darkness, where is the place thereof, **38:20** That thou shouldest take it to the bound thereof, and that thou shouldest know the paths to the house thereof? **38:21**

Knowest thou it, because thou wast then born? or because the number of thy days is great?

Did man create ice, hail and frost?

38:22 Hast thou entered into the treasures of the snow? or hast thou seen the treasures of the hail, **38:23** Which I have reserved against the time of trouble, against the day of battle and war?

Did man create rivers, rain, lightening or thunder?

38:24 By what way is the light parted, which scattereth the east wind upon the earth? **38:25** Who hath divided a watercourse for the overflowing of waters, or a way for the lightning of thunder; **38:26** To cause it to rain on the earth, where no man is; on the wilderness, wherein there is no man; **38:27** To satisfy the desolate and waste ground; and to cause the bud of the tender herb to spring forth?

What man designed and created the nature of water? Making the vapor, the rain, the frost and ice, or the dew?

38:28 Hath the rain a father? or who hath begotten the drops of dew? **38:29** Out of whose womb came the ice? and the hoary frost of heaven, who hath gendered it? **38:30** The waters are hid as with a stone, and the face of the deep is frozen.

Can man control the stars and bodies of the heavens like God did?

38:31 Canst thou bind the sweet influences of Pleiades, or loose the bands of Orion? **38:32** Canst thou bring forth Mazzaroth in his season? or canst thou guide Arcturus with his sons? **38:33** Knowest thou the ordinances of heaven? canst thou set the dominion thereof in the earth?

Can man command the rain?

38:34 Canst thou lift up thy voice to the clouds, that abundance of waters may cover thee? **38:35** Canst thou send lightnings, that they may go and say unto thee, Here we are?

Who created man and gave him understanding?

38:36 Who hath put wisdom in the inward parts? or who hath given understanding to the heart? **38:37** Who can number the clouds in wisdom? or who can stay the bottles of heaven, **38:38** When the dust groweth into hardness, and the clods cleave fast together?

Who set the instincts of the beasts?

38:39 Wilt thou hunt the prey for the lion? or fill the appetite of the young lions, **38:40** When they couch in their dens, and abide in the covert to lie in wait? **38:41** Who provideth for the raven his food? when his young ones cry unto God, they wander for lack of meat.

Who set in motion the systems of reproduction? It takes BOTH a female and a male to reproduce; it is impossible for that system to have evolved: Was this created by man; or by God to show his authorship of creation?

The Unicorn

Unicorns were not specific to Israel and are seen in the early writings and drawings of many different countries and cultures, including Greece, Persia (now Iran), Rome, Egypt, India and Africa.

The unicorn was chosen as a symbol of Scotland because of its traditional independence, virility, strength, boldness, masculinity and pride. The unicorn was first used on the Scottish royal coat of arms by William I in the 12th century. In the 15th century, when King James III was in power, gold coins appeared with the unicorn on them.

In 1603 king James 1 [in England, James VI of Scotland] added the Scottish unicorn to the lion of England. Then the term "strong bull" was deliberately mistranslated as "unicorn" by the king James I translators, to support the insertion of the modern symbol of Scotland [the unicorn] into the Bible; because he, a Scottish king, believed that he was a king of Israel from the line of David.

The Scottish unicorn like the English lion has nothing to do with a Davidic monarchy and is simply an elegant figure of royalty, pride and strength.

The **biblical** word "unicorn" and the **historical** "unicorn" are two completely different things.

The **historical** one horned unicorn is an ancient myth which is sourced from India and the rhino. This gradually became a mythical horse-like creature.

The **biblical** term "unicorn" is mistranslated from wild bull #7214 and speaks to the strength of a great wild bull which cannot be harnessed.

A translation error, when Hebrew scripture was rendered into Greek, added to the allure of the creature now known as the unicorn. The wild ox, a now-extinct creature rendered in bas relief [side view] profiles with one horn, was translated in Greek as monokeros or one-horned. In the Latin bible of the Christian world that word became unicornos and then "unicorn" by the time the English translators of King James got to work. And so, God impresses His power upon Job by saying, "Will the unicorn [great wild ox] be willing to serve thee, or abide by thy crib? Canst thou bind the unicorn with his band in the furrow? or will he harrow the valleys after thee?"

The word unicorn is found in nine places in the KJV, every one of which speaks of great strength and is a mistranslated reference to the now extinct great wild ox.

- **Numbers 23:22** "God brought them out of Egypt; he hath as it were the strength of an unicorn."
- **Numbers 24:8** "God brought him forth out of Egypt; he hath as it were the strength of an unicorn: he shall eat up the nations his enemies, and shall break their bones, and pierce them through with his arrows."
- **Job 39:9** "Will the unicorn be willing to serve thee, or abide by thy crib?"
- **Job 39:10** "Canst thou bind the unicorn with his band in the furrow? or will he harrow the valleys after thee?"
- **Psalms 29:6** "He maketh them also to skip like a calf; Lebanon and Sirion like a young unicorn."
- **Psalms 92:10** "But my horn shalt thou exalt like the horn of an unicorn: I shall be anointed with fresh oil."
- **Deuteronomy 33:17** "His glory is like the firstling of his bullock, and his horns are like the horns of unicorns: with them he shall push the people together to the ends of the earth: and they are the ten thousands of Ephraim, and they are the thousands of Manasseh."

- **Psalms 22:21** "Save me from the lion's mouth: for thou hast heard me from the horns of the unicorns."
- **Isaiah 34:7** "And the unicorns shall come down with them, and the bullocks with the bulls; and their land shall be soaked with blood, and their dust made fat with fatness."

Unicorns are not mentioned in any of the modern translations. Only in the King James version are they mentioned. Most of the modern translations say "wild ox." Some translations even say "buffalo," as in the Asian or African wild buffalo or water buffalo.

Job 39

Job 39:1 Knowest thou the time when the wild goats of the rock bring forth? or canst thou mark when the hinds do calve? **39:2** Canst thou number the months that they fulfil? or knowest thou the time when they bring forth? **39:3** They bow themselves, they bring forth their young ones, they cast out their sorrows [heaviness of pregnancy]. **39:4** Their young ones are in good liking, they grow up with corn [grain and grass]; they go forth, and return not unto them [their parents].

Who has made the wild creatures?

39:5 Who hath sent out the wild ass free? or who hath loosed the bands of the wild ass? **39:6** Whose house I have made the wilderness, and the barren land his dwellings. **39:7** He scorneth the multitude of the city, neither regardeth he the crying of the driver. **39:8** The range of the mountains is his pasture, and he searcheth after every green thing.

Can man make the wild ox to serve him?

39:9 Will the unicorn [an extinct ancient wild ox like creature] be willing to serve thee, or abide by thy crib? **39:10** Canst thou bind the unicorn with his band in the furrow? or will he harrow the valleys after thee? **39:11** Wilt thou trust him, because his strength is great? or wilt thou leave thy labour to him? **39:12** Wilt thou believe him, that he will bring home thy seed, and gather it into thy barn?

Brethren, did we make the beautiful birds, or the ostrich which scorns others yet she is foolish?

39:13 Gavest thou the goodly wings unto the peacocks? or wings and feathers unto the ostrich? **39:14** Which leaveth her eggs in the earth, and warmeth them in dust, **39:15** And forgetteth that the foot may crush them, or that the wild beast may break them. **39:16** She is hardened against her young ones, as though they were not her's: her labour is in vain without fear; **39:17** Because God hath deprived her of wisdom, neither hath he imparted to her understanding. **39:18** What time she lifteth up herself on high, she scorneth the horse and his rider.

Did man create the horse in his strength with his courage in battle?

39:19 Hast thou given the horse strength? hast thou clothed his neck with thunder? **39:20** Canst thou make him afraid as a grasshopper? the glory of his nostrils is terrible. **39:21** He paweth in the valley, and rejoiceth in his strength: he goeth on to meet the armed men. **39:22** He mocketh at fear, and is not affrighted; neither turneth he back from the sword. **39:23** The quiver rattleth against him, the glittering spear and the shield. **39:24** He swalloweth [covers the ground with speed] the ground with fierceness and rage: neither believeth he that it is the sound of the trumpet. **39:25** He saith among the trumpets, Ha, ha; and he smelleth the battle afar off, the thunder of the captains, and the shouting.

Has man created the birds of prey?

39:26 Doth the hawk fly by thy wisdom, and stretch her wings toward the south? **39:27** Doth the eagle mount up at thy command, and make her nest on high? **39:28** She dwelleth and abideth on the rock, upon the crag of the rock, and the strong place. **39:29** From thence she seeketh the prey, and her eyes behold afar off. **39:30** Her young ones also suck up blood: and where the slain are, there is she.

Job 40

God Corrects Job and All Those Who Justify Themselves

God now gets personal with Job and asks: who is man to justify himself before God?

Job 40:1 Moreover the LORD answered Job, and said, 40:2 Shall he that contendeth with the Almighty instruct him? he that reproveth God, let him answer it.

Job responds to God. Acknowledging his fault in justifying himself against God; yet today's Spiritual Ekklesia is full of sin and still justifies themselves before God, still needing to learn the same lesson that Job needed to learn.

40:3 Then Job answered the LORD, and said, 40:4 Behold, I am vile; what shall I answer thee? I will lay mine hand upon my mouth.

In his discussions with his friends Job has answered them once and then a second time; now he cannot answer God.

40:5 Once have I spoken; but I will not answer: yea, twice; but I will proceed no further.

God now instructs and rebukes Job for justifying himself. The day is close at hand when today's Spiritual Ekklesia will be corrected in our own tribulation.

40:6 Then answered the LORD unto Job out of the whirlwind, and said, **40:7** Gird up thy loins now like a man: I will demand of thee, and declare thou unto me.

40:8 Wilt thou also disannul my judgment? wilt thou condemn me, that thou mayest be righteous? 40:9 Hast thou an arm like God? or canst thou thunder with a voice like him?

Who are we to think that we can annul any part of God's Word or change [bind and loose] God's judgments? neither we nor Job can extricate ourselves out of God's correction of affliction, to raise ourselves up from the grave in glory; why then do we presume to justify ourselves in following men and not living by every Word of God?

40:10 Deck thyself now with majesty and excellency; and array thyself with glory and beauty.

This is also a reference to pride and how God is humbling Job and will humble us today.

40:11 Cast abroad the rage of thy wrath: and behold every one that is proud, and abase him. **40:12** Look on every one that is proud, and bring him low; and tread down the wicked in their place.

Are we equal with God? Can we truly justify and save ourselves?

40:13 Hide them in the dust together; and bind their faces in secret. **40:14** Then will I also confess unto thee that thine own right hand can save thee.

40:15 Behold now behemoth [possibly the elephant], which I made with thee; he eateth grass as an ox. **40:16** Lo now, his strength is in his loins, and his force is in the navel of his belly. **40:17** He moveth his tail like a cedar: the sinews of his stones are wrapped together. **40:18** His bones are as strong pieces of brass; his bones are like bars of iron. **40:19** He is the chief of the ways of God: [only] he that made him can make his sword to approach unto him.

40:20 Surely the mountains bring him forth food, where all the beasts of the field play. **40:21** He lieth under the shady trees, in the covert of the reed, and fens. **40:22** The shady trees cover him with their shadow; the willows of the brook compass him about. **40:23** Behold, he drinketh up a river, and hasteth not: he trusteth that he can draw up Jordan into his mouth. **40:24** He taketh it with his eyes: his nose [trunk] pierceth through snares.

Job 41

Job 41:1 Canst thou draw out leviathan [probably the giant salt water crocodile] with an hook? or his tongue with a cord which thou lettest down? **41:2** Canst thou put an hook into his nose? or bore his jaw through with a thorn? **41:3** Will he make many supplications unto thee? will he speak soft words unto thee? **41:4** Will he make a covenant with thee? wilt thou take him for a servant for ever? **41:5** Wilt thou play with him as with a bird? or wilt thou bind him for thy maidens? **41:6** Shall the companions make a banquet of him? shall they part him among the merchants? **41:7** Canst thou fill his skin with barbed irons? or his head with fish spears? **41:8** Lay thine hand upon him, remember the battle, do [it] no more. **41:9** Behold, the hope of him is in vain: shall not one be cast down even at the sight of him?

How then can a man justify himself against God?

41:10 None is so fierce that dare stir him up: **who then is able to stand before me? 41:11 Who** [can stop God] **hath prevented me, that I should repay him?** whatsoever is under the whole heaven is mine.

The man that is God's equal will be accepted as such by God; but what man is God's equal?

41:12 I will not conceal his parts, nor his power, nor his comely proportion.

Who can overcome the leviathan [probably the giant salt water crocodile, a type of Satan the dragon]? He has a very large mouth filled with very many strong teeth and his body is protected by strong scales. He rests in masses close together.

41:13 Who can discover the face of his garment? or who can come to him with his double bridle? **41:14** Who can open the doors of his face [his mouth is large]? his teeth are terrible round about. **41:15** His scales are his pride, shut up together as with a close seal. **41:16** One is so near to another, that no air can come between them. **41:17** They are joined one to another, they stick together, that they cannot be sundered.

41:18 By his neesings [sneezing, snorting] a light doth shine [the water foams], and his eyes are like the eyelids of the morning.

His expelling of air in the cool of the morning water appears like steam, and the bubbles in the water reflecting the dawn's light appear fiery.

41:19 Out of his mouth go burning lamps, and sparks of fire leap out. **41:20** Out of his nostrils goeth smoke [mist, steam], as out of a seething pot or caldron. **41:21** His breath [is like hot smoldering] kindleth coals, and a flame goeth out of his mouth.

By his great strength he takes whatever he wants.

41:22 In his neck remaineth strength, and sorrow is turned into joy before him. **41:23** The flakes of his flesh are joined together: they are firm in themselves; they cannot be moved. **41:24** His heart is as firm as a stone; yea, as hard as a piece of the nether millstone.

41:25 When he raiseth up himself, the mighty are afraid: by reason of [his breaking forth] breakings they purify themselves [they call on their gods in fear].

41:26 The sword of him that layeth at him cannot hold: the spear, the dart, nor the habergeon. **41:27** He esteemeth iron as straw, and brass as rotten wood. **41:28** The arrow cannot make him flee: slingstones are turned with him into stubble. **41:29** Darts are counted as stubble: he laugheth at the shaking of a spear. **41:30** Sharp stones are under him: he spreadeth sharp pointed things upon the mire.

41:31 [With his powerful taking of prey in the water] He maketh the deep to boil like a pot: he maketh the sea [to foam white and to look like] like a pot of ointment. **41:32** He maketh a [wake of water] path to shine after him; one would think the deep to be hoary. **41:33** Upon earth there is not his like, who is made without [he has no fear of anything] fear.

This animal is the king of the proud

41:34 He beholdeth all high things: he is a king over all the children of pride.

Job 42

Job repents and admits to speaking things that he did not understand. Just like today's Spiritual Ekklesia will also sincerely repent when we are corrected in great tribulation.

Job 42:1 Then Job answered the LORD, and said, **42:2** I know that thou canst do every thing, and that no thought can be withholden from thee. **42:3** Who is he that hideth counsel without knowledge? **therefore have I uttered that I understood not; things too wonderful for me, which I knew not.**

42:4 Hear, I beseech thee, and I will speak: I will demand of thee, and declare thou unto me. **42:5** I have heard of thee by the hearing of the ear: but now mine eye seeth thee.

Oh, that God would grant to all of us such sincere repentance: and God will bring today's Spiritual Ekklesia to such sincere repentance by the correction of great tribulation. Today's Spiritual Ekklesia will learn to stop justifying ourselves and to begin to live by every Word of Almighty God!!!

42:6 Wherefore I abhor myself, and repent in dust and ashes.

God then reprimands Job's three friends for speaking wrongly about God to Job, in not understanding that Job's problem was self-justification against God. Job had refused to sin against God in his affliction and yet he was accused of sin by his friends.

In fact Job had no sin **until be was afflicted and began to justify himself against God**, not understanding that God afflicts the righteous to complete their training as priests of the Most High.

The point of the sufferings of Job and Christ (as well as those of the saints) is to make them/us fit priests for mankind before God.

Notice that Christ was made a perfect high priest by that which He suffered and not by His sinless life. (Heb 2:10, Heb 5:8) From God's perspective it is important for a high priest to be both merciful and faithful (Heb 2:17-18).

The implications of Job's, our and Christ's sufferings, should also be obvious to all of the called of God throughout the ages. We are to become a "royal priesthood" (I Pet 2:9, Rev 1:6, Rev 5:10). We are to endure to the end of our physical lives. (Matt. 10:22) We are to suffer many afflictions from which God promises deliverance and ultimately great and abundant blessings. (Psalm 34:17-19)

Job wasn't being "punished" for any wrong. Job was being perfected for a very high office. God and Satan were not using Job as the object of some capricious argument over virtue,

God was using Satan, who for all his brilliance never did understand that he was being used as a tool for the perfecting of God's perfect holy priesthood.

42:7 And it was so, that after the LORD had spoken these words unto Job, the LORD said to Eliphaz the Temanite, My wrath is kindled against thee, and against thy two friends: for ye have not spoken of me the thing that is right, as my servant Job hath.

Job did not sin, except that he justified himself. When Job understood his folly he IMMEDIATELY REPENTED.

The situation is not the same today because today's called out are not nearly as righteous as Job was. Job was righteous and in his affliction began to sin by justifying himself; today we have strayed very far from God and are full of the sin of idolizing men above any zeal to live by every Word of God.

Righteous Job justified himself because he WAS righteous and could not see that God the Creator had the right to afflict his creation to perfect us.

Today's Spiritual Ekklesia who are indeed wicked, justify ourselves in exalting men, corporate entities and past false traditions above the Word of God!

Truly we are nowhere near as righteous as Job was, and we the sinful still try to justify ourselves in all our idolatries and sin!

Brethren, when we justify ourselves we deem ourselves righteous in our own eyes and therefore refuse to repent of our own ways; this is the sin unto death that cannot be pardoned by God.

> **John 5:16** If any man see his brother sin a sin which is not unto death, he shall ask, and he shall give him life for them that sin not unto death. There is a sin unto death [which is self-justification and a refusal to repent]: I do not say that he shall pray for it.

We have given a loving God no choice (Rev 3:16) except to correct us with a mighty correction, to humble us in the furnace of affliction and break us of the great sin of self-justification, in order to save us spiritually.

Without the correction of great tribulation we would carry on in unrepentant self-justification and refusing to repent we would receive the just wages of continued unrepented sin.

> **Romans 6:23** For the wages of sin is death; but the gift of God is eternal life through Jesus Christ our Lord.

The unpardonable sin, is the sin of self-justification and refusal to repent; and only God's loving and powerful correction can save many of today's brethren from this great sin and eternal death.

God is not willing that any should perish and he will bring us to understand and repent just like God saved Job; and after our correction ends with sincere repentance, God will raise us up in a resurrection to spirit with many other blessings!

Job 42:8 Therefore take unto you now seven bullocks and seven rams, and go to my servant Job, and offer up for yourselves a burnt offering; and my servant Job shall pray for you: for him will I accept: lest I deal with you after your folly, in that ye have not spoken of me the thing which is right, like my servant Job.

42:9 So Eliphaz the Temanite and Bildad the Shuhite and Zophar the Naamathite went, and did according as the LORD commanded them: the LORD also accepted Job.

God, then lifted the correction of Job and delivered him to far greater blessings!

God will also deliver all his sincerely repentant out of great tribulation and bless them greatly once they have learned the lesson to abhor self-justification and idolatry and turn to passionately live by every Word of God!

42:10 And the LORD turned the captivity of Job, when he prayed for his friends: also the LORD gave Job twice as much as he had before.

42:11 Then came there unto him all his brethren, and all his sisters, and all they that had been of his acquaintance before, and did eat bread with him in his house: and they bemoaned him, and comforted him over all the evil that the LORD had brought upon him: every man also gave him a piece of money, and every one an earring of gold.

42:12 So the LORD blessed the latter end of Job more than his beginning: for he had fourteen thousand sheep, and six thousand camels, and a thousand yoke of oxen, and a thousand she asses.

42:13 He had also seven sons and three daughters.

His new daughters were named:

 Jemima [a dove, peace with God. warmly affectionate: God is love],

 Keziah [Cassia spice: a symbol of the Wisdom of God] and

 Keren-Happuch [eye salve, eye ointment: God has opened my eyes].

42:14 And he called the name of the first, Jemima; and the name of the second, Kezia; and the name of the third, Kerenhappuch. **42:15** And in all the land were no women found so fair as the daughters of Job: and their father gave them inheritance among their brethren.

42:16 After this lived Job an hundred and forty years, and saw his sons, and his sons' sons, even four generations.

42:17 So Job died, being old and full of days.

Ecclesiastes

Introduction

The book of Deuteronomy is appointed to be read at the Feast of Tabernacles every seventh year (Deu 31:10). The Deuteronomy study can be found under the Deuteronomy Joshua title.

Ecclesiastes concerns the temporary transitory nature and pointlessness of physical things, teaching us that the only things that have lasting value are the eternal spiritual things of God.

The Book of Ecclesiastes was appointed to be read at the Feast of Tabernacles by Ezra and was probably written by Solomon, to be read during the Feast of Tabernacles.

Ecclesiastes is a lesson that all physical things ultimately end and that the only permanent things are spiritual, and that therefore we should be concerned with the spiritual as our priority. The lesson is that while we are to enjoy our physical lives, our focus should be on learning the spiritual lessons and principles that will bring the gift of eternal life and will last forever.

Those who have been called of God now, should be willing to give up everything physical for the spiritual gift of that pearl of great price, eternal life, seeking to internalize the nature of God through sincere repentance from all sin and a solid commitment to go forward to live by every Word of God.

If we dedicate ourselves to live by every Word of God in Christ-like zeal, using our physical lives to learn the spiritual things of God, then and only then will the sacrifice of the Lamb of God will be applied to us and the gift of God's Spirit will be given to enable us to become godly people.

The remainder of mankind who have not yet been called to God having their eyes opened to godliness, will after actual experience with life the first time around.

Then after dying and being resurrected back to physical life the main harvest of humanity will fully realize the temporary transitory nature of physical things, and will realize that only godliness has eternal and intrinsic lasting value.

Wiki: "Ecclesiastes takes its Hebrew name from the main speaker, Qoheleth, (also Koheleth), a word related to the root which means "to assemble". The idea behind the name was that probably the Teacher caused a group of students to assemble and hear his words; the Greek title is a modification of Ekklesia in an attempt to translate this, and the English is taken directly from the Greek. Qoheleth introduces himself as "son of David, king in Jerusalem," implying that he is Solomon.

The book is in the form of an autobiography, at times expressed in aphorisms and maxims, telling of his investigation into the meaning of life and the best way of life. The work emphatically proclaims all the actions of man to be inherently transitory, "vain", "futile", "empty", "meaningless", "temporary", "fleeting," or "mere breath," depending on translation, because the lives of both wise and foolish men end in death.

Qoheleth clearly endorses wisdom as a means for a well-lived earthly life, and the book is an instruction that the transitory nature of physical life, points us to the pressing need to seek the spiritual, while doing our best to enjoy the blessings God has provided in our present physical existence.

The teacher comes to this final conclusion: Let us hear the conclusion of the whole matter: Fear God, and keep his commandments: for this is the whole duty of man. (Ecc 12:13)."

The author Solomon was born to be king and grew up in his father's shadow, personally taught by a man after God's own heart, his own father king David, how to be a king.

When Solomon became king he asked God for wisdom as Solomon had been taught to seek wisdom above all else by his father David, and God respected that choice and also gave Solomon many other blessings.

Yet, Solomon had one big hole in his education, he had not grown up in adversity fleeing for his life like his father David had, or being imprisoned like Joseph, or working as a slave in Egypt; instead Solomon was born with the proverbial silver spoon.

Solomon had not learned to resist temptation or to persevere through trials; and as the years passed Solomon became infatuated with his own wisdom and slowly began to forget the commandments of God which are true wisdom. He began to make decisions based on what he thought looked right to him, and even the super-wise Solomon was NOT as wise as God and God's Word.

As Solomon began to rely on his own wisdom; he tried out and engaged in all manner of sin; and with the wisdom given him he began to understand the truth and ultimately came to repentance before God.

All of humanity is also being called [in their appointed times] to learn the same lesson, learning to deeply value, hunger and thirst after the spiritual things which are of far more value than gold or rubies because they will last forever.

The story of Solomon's journey to repentance is one of the most misunderstood Books of the Bible.

The Book of Ecclesiastes was written by a man of great wisdom, and in his experiences of his own ways, Solomon learns how little real meaning and lasting value physical things have in comparison to eternity, and the wisdom of God's Word; and he comes to a place of repentance.

Living by every Word of God is the ONLY way that brings eternal life.

We MUST learn the lesson that only by internalizing the very nature of God through faithfully living by every Word of God can we live forever as God lives forever.

When we repent of living contrary to the Word of God or compromising with even the very least commandment, and we then commit to live by every Word of God forever [which is what baptism is]; only then will the sacrifice of the Lamb of God Jesus Christ be applied to us, atoning for PAST sins, reconciling us to God the Father and bringing the birthright of eternal life.

Only when we learn the lesson that Solomon learned, that the purpose of physical existence is to provide an environment for learning spiritual lessons and principles, and then we dedicate ourselves to godliness, will we be fit to receive the gift of eternal life.

Ecclesiastes 12:13 Let us hear the conclusion of the whole matter: Fear God, and keep his commandments: for this is the whole duty of man. **12:14** For God shall bring every work into judgment, with every secret thing, whether it be good, or whether it be evil.

Solomon

- **WIKI** "Solomon (Hebrew: שְׁלֹמֹה, Modern *Shlomo* Tiberian *Šəlōmō* ISO 259-3 *Šlomo*; Arabic: سليمان *Sulaymān*, also colloquially: *Silimān*; Greek: Σολομών *Solomōn*), also called **Jedidiah** (Hebrew יְדִידְיָה), was, according to the Book of Kings and the Book of Chronicles, a king of Israel and the son of David. The conventional dates of Solomon's reign are circa 970 to 931 BC. He is described as the third king of the United Monarchy, and the final king before the northern Kingdom of Israel and the southern Kingdom of Judah split. Following the split, his patrilineal descendants ruled over Judah alone.

Solomon was loved by God from his birth:"

2 Samuel 12:24 And David comforted Bathsheba his wife, and went in unto her, and lay with her: and she bare a son, and he called his name Solomon: and the Lord loved him. **12:25** And he sent by the hand of Nathan the prophet; and he called his name Jedidiah [meaning "Beloved of YHVH"], because of the Lord.

Solomon had been made heir apparent in his youth; probably because he was the son of Bathsheba David's favorite, and probably because Solomon was diligent to learn of God and God's commandments from his father David. The Eternal did not call Solomon his beloved as a young child for nothing; the child must have been faithful and diligent learning of God from David his father, as David educated him to become king over Israel.

1 Kings 1:11 Wherefore Nathan [the prophet] spake unto Bathsheba the mother of Solomon, saying, Hast thou not heard that Adonijah the son of Haggith doth reign, and David our lord knoweth it not?

1:12 Now therefore come, let me, I pray thee, give thee counsel, that thou mayest save thine own life, and the life of thy son Solomon.

1:13 Go and get thee in unto king David, and say unto him, **Didst not thou, my lord, O king, swear unto thine handmaid, saying, Assuredly Solomon thy son shall reign after me, and he shall sit upon my throne?** why then doth Adonijah reign?

1:14 Behold, **while thou yet talkest there with the king, I also will come in after thee, and confirm thy words.**

When Solomon became king and had secured the realm he proposed to build a House for God as his father David had wanted [I have no doubt that they discussed this often together, and made plans together; for David laid up a vast sum for Solomon to build with.]. Solomon was full of love for God and his Word; having been zealous for these things from his birth.

At about that time, God who loved Solomon for his love of God's law from childhood, offered Solomon a blessing, and Solomon being humble before God, as taught by David; asked for wisdom to rule God's people.

Psalm 111:1 The fear of the Lord is the beginning of wisdom: a good understanding have all they that do his commandments: his praise endureth for ever.

Solomon had been taught the fear and love of God by his father David.

God granted this request and further blessed Solomon with many other things, for wisdom has her fruits.

Solomon started his rule, very wise in the things and commandments of God, however he began to slowly lose his humility and be ensnared by pride.

Solomon then set out to test God and God's Word, and to test also his own wisdom and ways, by considering everything that this world has to offer and judging physical things for their real value.

The Book of Ecclesiastes is about what Solomon learned from his testing and inquiries into all the greatness that this world has to offer.

Ecclesiastes is about pride or humility, worldliness or godliness; and about transitory physical things without lasting value or spiritual things which have true lasting eternal value.

This book is very, very, vital to those claiming to be God's people today. God deeply loved Solomon and therefore allowed Solomon to make his mistakes and learn from them.

The same is true today; God deeply loves all his called out, and he is allowing us to do what we think is right so we may make our mistakes and learn from them, in order to perfect us so that we might be zealous for all eternity!

Oh, how God has loved us, but very many of us are like rebellious children, preferring our own wisdom to the wisdom of God our Father; preferring our own ways and traditions to the truth and commandments of our loving Father.

God is warning his beloved children of the way that they should go, and we had better heed his warning, before we are destroyed by the wisdom of men and the traditions of men.

Ecclesiastes was written at the end of Solomon's inquiries, and was inspired by God to teach us the same lesson that Solomon learned; so that we might come to the same conclusion as Solomon; and dedicate ourselves to the ONLY things that really matter and have lasting value; God and his commandments.

The lessons of Ecclesiastes are an analogy of humanity who try out all their own ways to finally learn that only that the ways of God are all that is truly permanent and all that really matters. Some will learn this lesson now while the vast majority of mankind will understand these things when they are raised up to physical life and God opens their eyes to spiritual understanding in the main Feast of Tabernacles harvest of humanity.

Ecclesiastes 1

Ecclesiastes 1:1 The words of the Preacher, the son of David, king in Jerusalem.

After deep and lengthy study, the Teacher emphatically proclaims all the actions of man to be inherently *hevel*, a word meaning "vain", "futile", "empty", "meaningless", "temporary", "transitory", "fleeting," or "mere breath," depending on translation, as the lives of both wise and foolish men end in death.

Why do men seek physical fame, power or wealth in this life? Why do they seek their own ways which are vanity and will come to nothing, and reject the truth of God?

1:2 Vanity of vanities, saith the Preacher, vanity of vanities; all is vanity.
1:3 What profit hath a man of all his labour which he taketh under the sun?
1:4 One generation passeth away, and another generation cometh: but the earth abideth for ever.

Physical things never satisfy for long.

1:5 The sun also ariseth, and the sun goeth down, and hasteth to his place where he arose. **1:6** The wind goeth toward the south, and turneth about unto the north; it whirleth about continually, and the wind returneth again according to his circuits. **1:7** All the rivers run into the sea; yet the sea is not full; unto the place from whence the rivers come, thither they return again. **1:8** All things are full of labour; man cannot utter it: the eye is not satisfied with seeing, nor the ear filled with hearing.

Physical thing do not last and never satisfy for long.

1:9 The thing that hath been, it is that which shall be; and that which is done is that which shall be done: and there is no new thing under the sun. **1:10** Is there any thing whereof it may be said, See, this is new? it hath been already of old time, which was before us. **1:11** There is no remembrance of former things; neither shall there be any remembrance of things that are to come with those that shall come after.

The Preacher or Instructor in Wisdom, is identified as king Solomon.

1:12 I the Preacher **was king over Israel in Jerusalem**.

Solomon seeks out the meaning of life, and seeks out wisdom concerning all things physical. He seeks out all the wisdom and pleasures of man, as many others before and after him have done.

1:13 And I gave my heart to seek and search out by wisdom concerning all things that are done under heaven: this sore travail hath God given to the sons of man to be exercised therewith.

Solomon learns what all people will eventually learn; that there is nothing lasting or satisfying in this very temporary physical existence; ONLY the things of God are permanent and satisfying.

1:14 I have seen all the works that are done under the sun; and, behold, all is vanity and vexation of spirit. **1:15** That which is crooked cannot be made straight: and that which is wanting cannot be numbered.

Solomon sought out wisdom and realized that human wisdom is vexation and madness, for wisdom reveals the emptiness and futility of physical existence.

1:16 I communed with mine own heart, saying, Lo, I am come to great estate, and have gotten more wisdom than all they that have been before me in Jerusalem: yea, my heart had great experience of wisdom and knowledge. **1:17** And I gave my heart to know wisdom, and to know madness and folly: I perceived that this also is vexation of spirit.

When we understand that we shall all surely die and our existence will end, all other things become empty, meaningless and hopeless folly.

1:18 For in much wisdom is much grief: and he that increaseth knowledge increaseth sorrow.

Solomon then seeks out wealth and the pleasures of life to see if he will find meaning there.

Ecclesiastes 2

Solomon sought to find meaning in life through pleasure seeking because wisdom revealed that he would eventually die and cease to exist anyway.

Ecclesiastes 2:1 I said in mine heart, Go to now, I will prove thee with mirth, therefore enjoy pleasure: and, behold, this also is vanity.

Solomon then learned that pleasure seeking is pointless and ultimately proves to be empty and meaningless.

2:2 I said of laughter, It is mad: and of mirth, What doeth it? **2:3** I sought in mine heart to give myself unto wine, yet acquainting mine heart with wisdom; and to lay hold on folly, till I might see what was that good for the sons of men, which they should do under the heaven all the days of their life.

Then he sought riches and building projects, only to find them ultimate meaningless as all physical things will ultimately perish.

2:4 I made me great works; I builded me houses; I planted me vineyards: **2:5** I made me gardens and orchards, and I planted trees in them of all kind of fruits: **2:6** I made me pools of water, to water therewith the wood that bringeth forth trees:

2:7 I got me servants and maidens, and had servants born in my house; also I had great possessions of great and small cattle above all that were in Jerusalem before me:

2:8 I gathered me also silver and gold, and the peculiar treasure of kings and of the provinces: I gat me men singers and women singers, and the delights of the sons of men, as musical instruments, and that of all sorts.

2:9 So I was great, and increased more than all that were before me in Jerusalem: also my wisdom remained with me.

2:10 And whatsoever mine eyes desired I kept not from them, I withheld not my heart from any joy; for my heart rejoiced in all my labour: and this was my portion of all my labour.

2:11 Then I looked on all the works that my hands had wrought, and on the labour that I had laboured to do: and, behold, all was vanity and vexation of spirit, and there was no profit under the sun.

Solomon tests wisdom against foolishness.

2:12 And I turned myself to behold wisdom, and madness, and folly: for what can the man do that cometh after the king? even that which hath been already done.

Wisdom is far greater than foolishness, yet what is its advantage at the end of physical life?

2:13 Then I saw that wisdom excelleth folly, as far as light excelleth darkness.

2:14 The wise man's eyes [are open see and understand] are in his head; but the fool walketh in darkness: and I myself perceived also that one event happeneth to them all.

Then Solomon understood that both the humanly wise and the foolish die and cease to exist.

2:15 Then said I in my heart, As it happeneth to the fool, so it happeneth even to me; and why was I then more wise? Then I said in my heart, that this also is vanity.

2:16 For there is no remembrance of the wise more than of the fool for ever; seeing that which now is in the days to come shall all be forgotten. And how dieth the wise man? as the fool.

Solomon learns that at the end of life, the age old question remains: "Is that all there is?" If so then life itself is foolishness for it has no lasting value.

2:17 Therefore I hated life; because the work that is wrought under the sun is grievous unto me: for all is vanity and vexation of spirit.

Solomon despairs that his heirs will be successful to maintain his projects.

2:18 Yea, I hated all my labour which I had taken under the sun: because I should leave it unto the man that shall be after me. **2:19** And who knoweth whether he shall be a wise man or a fool? yet shall he have rule over all my labour wherein I have laboured, and wherein I have shewed myself wise under the sun. This is also vanity.

2:20 Therefore I went about to cause my heart to despair of all the labour which I took under the sun.

Solomon learns that all physical pursuits are empty and meaningless and loses all desire to pursue them further.

Solomon despairs as he realizes that the fruits of all his wisdom and labours will ultimate be left to another who probably does not deserve it and will make a big mess of them.

2:21 For there is a man whose labour is in wisdom, and in knowledge, and in equity; yet to a man that hath not laboured therein shall he leave it for his portion. This also is vanity and a great evil.

What has a man left for himself of all his labours when he dies?

2:22 For what hath man of all his labour, and of the vexation of his heart, wherein he hath laboured under the sun? **2:23** For all his days are sorrows, and his travail grief; yea, his heart taketh not rest in the night. This is also vanity.

Therefore in physical things, people should enjoy life to the full while they still live. Let men enjoy the fruits of their labours.

2:24 There is nothing better for a man, than that he should eat and drink, and that he should make his soul enjoy good in his labour. This also I saw, that it was from the hand of God. **2:25** For who can eat, or who else can hasten hereunto, more than I?

The wicked build up, so that God will take from them and give to the righteous. Therefore it is vexation [empty foolishness] of spirit to be wicked and break God's commandments. Those who compromise with God's commandments or teach tolerance for sin are foolish vain and spiritual empty men.

2:26 For God giveth to a man that is good in his [God's] sight wisdom, and knowledge, and joy: but to the sinner he giveth travail, to gather and to heap up, that he may give to him that is good before God. This also is vanity and vexation of spirit.

Ecclesiastes 3

There is a right time for everything and often patience is in order

Ecclesiastes 3:1 To every thing there is a season, and a time to every purpose under the heaven: **3:2** A time to be born, and a time to die; a time to plant, and a time to pluck up that which is planted;

3:3 A time to kill, and a time to heal; a time to break down, and a time to build up; **3:4** A time to weep, and a time to laugh; a time to mourn, and a time to dance;

3:5 A time to cast away stones, and a time to gather stones together; a time to embrace, and a time to refrain from embracing; **3:6** A time to get, and a time to lose; a time to keep, and a time to cast away;

3:7 A time to rend, and a time to sew; a time to keep silence, and a time to speak; **3:8** A time to love, and a time to hate; a time of war, and a time of peace.

The law may allow something, but it is not always expedient to do what the law allows. Wisdom must be exercised in what we do, even regarding lawful things. Carefully choose the right time and place for all your doings, so as to prosper in them.

What profit is there in our labours, except to take pleasure and be satisfied with our work? And to rejoice and enjoy its fruits.

3:9 What profit hath he that worketh in that wherein he laboureth? **3:10** I have seen the travail, which God hath given to the sons of men to be exercised in it.

No carnally minded person whose thoughts are on physical pursuits, can understand the works and Word of God.

3:11 He [God] hath made every thing beautiful in his time: also he hath set the world [worldliness and limited understanding to the carnal man] in their heart, so that no man can find out the work that God maketh from the beginning to the end.

3:12 I know that there is no good in them [worldliness and physical pursuits], but for a man to rejoice, and to do good [keep the commandments of God] in his life.

All good things including the fruits of our own labour and wisdom, are gifts of God, for he has made and sustains all things.

3:13 And also that every man should eat and drink, and enjoy the good of all his labour, it is the gift of God.

Only the godly things are eternal and have any real meaning, and no person can change what God has ordained. Men should fear God for only he is eternal and is of any importance in the larger scheme of things.

3:14 I know that, whatsoever God doeth, it shall be for ever: nothing can be put to it, nor any thing taken from it: and God doeth it, that men should fear before him. **3:15** That which hath been is now; and that which is to be hath already been; and God requireth that which is past.

Solomon saw that there was unequal justice and wickedness in the judgment and ruler-ship of men. And that in the physical priesthood and temple there was sin. Therefore man can only count on God for righteous judgment.

3:16 And moreover I saw under the sun the place of judgment, that wickedness was there; and the place of righteousness, that iniquity was there. **3:17** I said in mine heart, God shall judge the righteous and the wicked: for there is a time there for every purpose and for every work.

At God's judgments, God shall demonstrate that physical man is as the brute beasts who cannot understand. Therefore only the spiritual things and commandments of God have any value or really matter.

3:18 I said in mine heart concerning the estate of the sons of men, that God might manifest them, and that they might see that they themselves are beasts.

3:19 For that which befalleth the sons of men befalleth beasts; even one thing befalleth them: as the one dieth, so dieth the other; yea, they have all one breath; so that a man hath no preeminence above a beast: for all is vanity. **3:20** All go unto one place; all are of the dust, and all turn to dust again.

3:21 Who knoweth the spirit [Reuach, spirit, breath] of man that goeth upward, and the spirit [Reuach, spirit, breath] of the beast that goeth downward to the earth?

Serve God in the wisdom of God's Word and enjoy life to the full, for after death all our physical deeds and wealth will go to another.

3:22 Wherefore I perceive that there is nothing better, than that a man should rejoice in his own works; for that is his portion: for who shall bring him to see what shall be after him?

Solomon considers the state of man, between the oppressed and the oppressors.

Ecclesiastes 4

Ecclesiastes 4:1 So I returned, and considered all the oppressions that are done under the sun: and behold the tears of such as were oppressed, and they had no comforter; and on the side of their oppressors there was power; but they had no comforter.

It is better to be dead than to be oppressed and without relief.

4:2 Wherefore I praised the dead which are already dead more than the living which are yet alive.

The person who has not seen oppression or been an oppressor, is blessed to have been saved from exposure to such evil.

4:3 Yea, better is he [who has never seen evil and oppression] than both they [the oppressed and the oppressor], [better is the one who has not yet been born or seen such evil] which hath not yet been, who hath not seen the evil work that is done under the sun.

Solomon now considers the labours of men. Great and good accomplishments that make men famous, are pointless without God, because in the end they will come to nothing.

4:4 Again, I considered all travail [work, labour, trials], and every right work, that for this a man is envied of his neighbour. This is also vanity and vexation of spirit.

Yet, it is foolishness to be lazy and do nothing.

4:5 The fool foldeth his hands together, and eateth his own flesh.

It is better to have little, accompanied by peace and peace of mind; than to have much and be in interminable strife and stress.

4:6 Better is an handful with quietness, than both the hands full with travail and vexation of spirit.

4:7 Then I returned, and I saw vanity under the sun.

Greed for physical wealth is a sore and heavy burden, working men to death; and has no reward for all perish in the end.

4:8 There is one alone, and there is not a second; yea, he hath neither child nor brother: yet is there no end of all his labour; neither is his eye satisfied with riches; neither saith he, For whom do I labour, and bereave my soul of good? This is also vanity, yea, it is a sore travail.

It is better to work together with others.

4:9 Two are better than one; because they have a good reward for their labour. **4:10** For if they fall, the one will lift up his fellow: but woe to him that is alone when he falleth; for he hath not another to help him up.

4:11 Again, if two lie together, then they have heat: but how can one be warm alone? **4:12** And if one prevail against him, two shall withstand him; and a threefold cord is not quickly broken.

The following is especially true spiritually, for the Ekklesia is now full of old and foolish rulers who will not be admonished, while the kingdom of God shall be filled with the wisdom of faithful obedient children.

> **Matthew 18:2** And Jesus called a little child unto him, and set him in the midst of them,

18:3 And said, Verily I say unto you, Except ye be converted, and become as little children [humble and trusting in God], ye shall not enter into the kingdom of heaven.

18:4 Whosoever therefore shall humble himself as this little child, the same is greatest in the kingdom of heaven.

Ecclesiastes 4:13 Better is a poor and a wise child than an old and foolish king, who will no more be admonished.

The commandment breaking ruler, leader or elder; is foolish and imprisoned by wickedness, all his subjects will suffer for his wickedness.

4:14 For out of prison he cometh to reign; whereas also he that is born in his kingdom becometh poor.

The righteous obedient child shall grow up to take the ruler-ship from the foolish leader.

4:15 I considered all the living which walk under the sun, with the second child that shall stand up in his stead.

It is foolishness, not to rejoice in God and his commandments; for the physical works of men shall not be long remembered. The accomplishments of the mighty shall not long be remembered after their death.

4:16 There is no end of all the people, even of all that have been before them: they also that come after shall not rejoice in him. Surely this also is vanity and vexation of spirit.

Seek out the wisdom of God in his Word; rather than teaching what we do not really know and understand. The student should study and not teach until he is fully and properly prepared in his studies by inspiration of God.

Be very careful in your prayers and petitions to God. It is vanity and foolishness to pray for an hour each day, just to waste God's time with much speaking.

Make your prayers sincere and from the heart, and do not engage in empty ramblings to put in time. Better is a prayer of three minutes from the heart, than hours of empty words.

Ecclesiastes 5

It is far better to listen, learn and keep the whole Word of God, than to foolishly commit sin and be required to offer sacrifices for sin.

Ecclesiastes 5:1 Keep thy foot when thou goest to the house of God, and be more ready to hear, than to give the sacrifice of fools: for they consider not that they do evil.

Think before you speak and do not be over quick to answer a matter without thinking.

5:2 Be not rash with thy mouth, and let not thine heart be hasty to utter any thing before God: for God is in heaven, and thou upon earth: therefore let thy words be few. **5:3** For a dream cometh through the multitude of business [an active mind]; and a fool's voice is known by multitude of [empty] words.

5:4 When thou vowest a vow unto God, defer not to pay it; for he hath no pleasure in fools: pay that which thou hast vowed. **5.5** Better is it that thou shouldest not vow, than that thou shouldest vow and not pay.

Do not make promises to God, lest you fail to keep them, for if you make a promise to God, Satan will immediately work to make keeping your word a heavy burden to you. Instead fear God and do HIS will, making no promises to God, except for your baptismal marriage commitment.

5:6 Suffer not thy mouth to cause thy flesh to sin; neither say thou before the angel, that it was an error: wherefore should God be angry at thy voice, and destroy the work of thine hands? **5:7** For in the multitude of dreams and many words there are also divers vanities: but fear thou God.

You oppressors of the flock; you shall be judged of God.

5:8 If thou seest the oppression of the poor, and violent perverting of judgment and justice in a province, marvel not at the matter: for he that is higher than the highest regardeth; and there be higher than they [A higher one than the evil doer, who shall judge him.].

All things come out of the earth that God has made for humanity. Therefore all that humanity has, is a gift of God without which we could not even exist.

5:9 Moreover the profit of the earth is for all: the king himself is served by the field.

No matter what physical thing man desires, when he has achieved it; he will not be satisfied with it. for physical things are not of any real value; only the spiritual is satisfying and everlasting.

5:10 He that loveth silver shall not be satisfied with silver; nor he that loveth abundance with increase: this is also vanity.

What is the point of acquiring more than we can use; except to help others. Let the rich be generous to the poor and they will see treasures laid up for them in heaven.

5:11 When goods increase, they are increased that eat them: and what good is there to the owners thereof, saving the beholding of them with their eyes?

5:12 The sleep of a labouring man is sweet, whether he eat little or much: but the abundance of the rich will not suffer him to sleep.

5:13 There is a sore evil which I have seen under the sun, namely, riches kept for the owners thereof to their hurt.

5:14 But those riches perish by evil travail: and he begetteth a son, and there is nothing in his hand [there is nothing laid up for him in heaven when he dies].

Physical wealth is of no real lasting value, only the spiritual has lasting value. Those who seek the pleasures and wealth of this world shall die and have nothing laid up in heaven for themselves. it is better to do good and keep God's commandments always, then to lust after worldliness.

5:15 As he came forth of his mother's womb, naked shall he return to go as he came, and shall take nothing of his labour, which he may carry away in his hand.

5:16 And this also is a sore evil, that in all points as he came, so shall he go: and what profit hath he that hath laboured for the wind?

5:17 All his days also he eateth in darkness, and he hath much sorrow and wrath with his sickness.

Enjoy life and help others as God blesses you; but do not set your heart on ungodly lusts and pleasures.

5:18 Behold that which I have seen: it is good and comely for one to eat and to drink, and to enjoy the good of all his labour that he taketh under the sun all the days of his life, which God giveth him: for it is his portion.

Let us use what God has given us for godly purposes and keep his commandments always.

5:19 Every man also to whom God hath given riches and wealth, and hath given him power to eat thereof, and to take his portion, and to rejoice in his labour; this is the gift of God.

5:20 For he shall not much remember the days of his life; because God answereth him in the joy of his heart.

It is a sore burden to work hard and then have one's reward taken by another; in usury and taxes, or by fraud or theft, or by cunning words.

Ecclesiastes 6

Ecclesiastes 6:1 There is an evil which I have seen under the sun, and it is common among men:

6:2 A man to whom God hath given riches, wealth, and honour, so that he wanteth nothing for his soul of all that he desireth, yet God giveth him not power to eat thereof, but a stranger eateth it: this is vanity, and it is an evil disease.

If a man work hard all his life and enjoy none of it, and if he has not laid up a reward in heaven; it is a great evil.

6:3 If a man beget an hundred children, and live many years, so that the days of his years be many, and his soul be not filled with good, and also that he have no burial; I say, that an untimely [miscarried] birth is better than he.

6:4 For he cometh in with vanity, and departeth in darkness, and his name shall be covered with darkness.

6:5 Moreover he [that has not been born being miscarried and] hath not seen the sun, nor known any thing: this hath more rest than the other.

If a man is rich in physical things, and not knowing God or keeping his commandments, lives for a thousand years; he will still die; the physically rich, or carnally wise; shall still die, like the fool.

The ONLY things that has any real lasting value, are the commandments and teachings of God and our relationship with the Father and the Son!

6:6 Yea, though he live a thousand years twice told, yet hath he seen no [true good thing] good: do not all go to one place?

6:7 All the labour of man is for his mouth, and yet the appetite is not filled.

6:8 For what hath the wise more than the fool? what hath the poor, that knoweth to walk before the living?

It is better to have, than to desire and not have.

6:9 Better is the sight of the eyes than the wandering of the desire: this is also vanity and vexation of spirit.

Man cannot contend with God; it is better to keep God's Words and ways than to perish in foolishness.

6:10 That which hath been is named already, and it is known that it is man: neither may he contend with him that is mightier than he.

The day of death of the righteous, is in conscious thought, the day of his birth into the Family of God, therefore it is better than the beginning of his life and physical sorrows at his physical birth. The same is true of the unconverted, for they shall have a new life in the main harvest into the Family of God.

6:11 Seeing there be many things that increase vanity, what is man the better?

6:12 For who knoweth what is good for man in this life, all the days of his vain life which he spendeth as a shadow? for who can tell a man what shall be after him under the sun? [Only God!]

Ecclesiastes 7

A Few Proverbs

A good reputation is priceless, however there are many in this evil world who will lie, or use innuendo to destroy good names. Their deceitful work is in vain, for God will bring the truth out in his good time.

Ecclesiastes 7:1 A good name is better than precious ointment; and the day of death than the day of one's birth.

Mourning a loss helps put life in its proper perspective and bring us to God. Reveling in carnal events only encourages our carnal nature towards more worldliness and personal pride.

Sadness turns us to understand that the only things of real consequence are the things of God; therefore mourning brings us back to a good understanding of the transitory nature of the physical and the need for God.

7:2 It is better to go to the house of mourning, than to go to the house of feasting: for that is the end of all men; and the living will lay it to his heart.

7:3 Sorrow is better than laughter: for by the sadness of the countenance the heart is made better.

7:4 The heart of the wise is in the house of mourning [repentance]; but the heart of fools is in the house of mirth.

The correction of God's Word is better than precious jewels to the one who responds positively and corrects himself.

7:5 It is better to hear the rebuke of the wise, than for a man to hear the song of fools.

The joy of those who break God's law and compromise with God's commandments is the sound of fools running to their own destruction.

7:6 For as the crackling of thorns under a pot, so is the laughter of the fool: this also is vanity.

The godly man hates oppression, and a bribe destroys the righteousness of the godly.

The heart is representative of our nature and a bribe is a desire for physical wealth above well doing in keeping all of God's commandments.

7:7 Surely oppression maketh a wise man mad; and a gift destroyeth the heart.

It is better to have successfully completed a project, then to be only beginning and possible fail.

7:8 Better is the end of a thing than the beginning thereof: and the patient in spirit is better than the proud in spirit.

Control your temper and suppress and control anger; for an uncontrolled temper leads to much shame and evil.

7:9 Be not hasty in thy spirit to be angry: for anger resteth in the bosom of fools.

7:10 Say not thou, What is the cause that the former days were better than these? for thou dost not enquire wisely concerning this.

The greatest inheritance that a parent can give is wise instruction of his children, and the wise person who also inherits wealth with wisdom, will do much good with it.

7:11 Wisdom is good with an inheritance: and by it there is profit to them that see the sun.

7:12 For wisdom is a defence, and money is a defence: but the excellency of knowledge is, that wisdom giveth life to them that have it.

Do not oppose God in his will, for he gives blessings and takes them away, to teach us the vanity of all physical things.

7:13 Consider the work of God: for who can make that straight, which he hath made crooked?

7:14 In the day of prosperity be joyful, but in the day of adversity consider: God also hath set the one over against the other, to the end that man should find nothing after him.

Solomon now gets into self-righteousness and the pointlessness of man following the righteousness of men; by doing what he thinks is right, instead of doing what God commands.

7:15 All things have I seen in the days of my vanity: there is a just man that perisheth in his righteousness, and there is a wicked man that prolongeth his life in his wickedness.

Justice or wickedness according to the thoughts of what is right to a man, means nothing in the end; for both what appears just or evil to humanity will fail [men think that abortion and much wickedness is right]. It is those who fear God and are just, by the keeping of all of God's commandments, who have something of real value for eternity.

Therefore be not self-righteous, nor worldly wise; instead be godly righteous and godly wise, through the diligent keeping of all of his teachings and commandments.

This verse has been badly twisted by the wicked, who declare the zealous for God over righteous, when the verse is actually about the SELF-RIGHTEOUSNESS of the wicked, who are zealous for their OWN ways and NOT zealous for the ways of God.

7:16 Be not righteous over much; neither make thyself over wise: why shouldest thou destroy thyself?

Do not depart from zeal for God and his Word like the wicked.

7:17 Be not over much wicked, neither be thou foolish: why shouldest thou die before thy time?

7:18 It is good that thou shouldest take hold of this; yea, also from this withdraw not thine hand: **for he that feareth God shall come forth of them all.**

A wise man is better than ten strong men who dissipate their strength in foolishness.

7:19 Wisdom strengtheneth the wise more than ten mighty men which are in the city.

> **Romans 3:23** For all have sinned, and come short of the glory of God;

Therefore let us look to God and not to men for righteousness.

Ecclesiastes 7:20 For there is not a just man upon earth, that doeth good, and sinneth not.

Do not eves drop or be so thin skinned and over sensitive that you take exception to every critical word. Learn to let little things slide or your life will be miserable and full of vexations.

7:21 Also take no heed unto all words that are spoken; lest thou hear thy servant curse thee:

7:22 For oftentimes also thine own heart knoweth that thou thyself likewise hast cursed others.

Solomon proved out these things by wise thought, but found little understanding of the things of God by human wisdom.

7:23 All this have I proved by wisdom: I said, I will be wise; but it was far from me.

Solomon found that the greatest evil to befall him was the enticements of wicked women who made his life a misery and were his downfall. In this he was speaking of his own desire for strange [unconverted] women.

The righteous man should seek out a righteous woman. This is true of Christ for he will not marry an unclean by sin bride.

7:24 That which is far off, and exceeding deep, who can find it out?

7:25 I applied mine heart to know, and to search, and to seek out wisdom, and the reason of things, and to know the wickedness of folly, even of foolishness and madness:

7:26 And I find more bitter than death the woman, whose heart is snares and nets, and her hands as bands: **whoso pleaseth God shall escape from her; but the sinner shall be taken by her.**

7:27 Behold, this have I found, saith the preacher [teacher], counting one by one, to find out the account:

7:28 Which yet my soul seeketh, but I find not [any righteous]: one [righteous] man among a thousand have I found; but a [good] woman among all those have I not found.

7:29 Lo, this only have I found, that God hath made man [to be] upright [godly]; but they have sought out many [wicked] inventions.

Ecclesiastes 8

A wise man respects authority and submits to the ruler, beginning with God; and then the rulers of the nations.

Ecclesiastes 8:1 Who is as the wise man? and who knoweth the interpretation of a thing? a man's wisdom maketh his face to shine, and the boldness of his face shall be changed.

We should keep the commandment of the physical king because he exercises physical power over us! How much more should we keep the commandments of the King of kings who has power of eternal life and death?

8:2 I counsel thee to keep the king's commandment, and that in regard of the oath of God.

8:3 Be not hasty to go out of his [to try and hide from the king's sight, by extension to leave the presence of God; in order to do evil] sight: stand not in an evil thing; for he doeth whatsoever pleaseth him.

8:4 Where the word of a king [God the Father is King of the universe and Christ is King over the earth] is, there is power: and who may say unto him, What doest thou?

8:5 Whoso keepeth the commandment [of God who is the ultimate King] shall feel no evil thing: and a wise man's heart discerneth both time and judgment.

Man has no power to achieve eternal life; which is the gift of God the King of those who obey him.

8:6 Because to every purpose there is time and judgment, therefore the misery of man is great upon him. **8:7** For he knoweth not that which shall be: for who can tell him when it shall be?

8:8 There is no man that hath power over the spirit to retain the spirit; neither hath he power in the day of death: and there is no discharge in that war; neither shall wickedness deliver those that are given to it.

Men rule over others, dominating and abusing; not believing that God rules over them and will call them to account.

8:9 All this have I seen, and applied my heart unto every work that is done under the sun: there is a time wherein one man ruleth over another to his own hurt.

All men die and there is no profit in the gain of the wicked. Let us obey our God and he shall give the gift of eternal life.

8:10 And so I saw the wicked buried, who had come and gone from the place of the holy, and they were forgotten in the city where they had so done: this is also vanity.

Because there seems to be no immediate bad result of much evil, short sighted men do not see the consequences of their evil deeds.

8:11 Because sentence against an evil work is not executed speedily, therefore the heart of the sons of men is fully set in them to do evil.

God's gift of eternal life in peace is reserved for those who love him and keep his commandments, while the end of the commandment breaker is his destruction.

8:12 Though a sinner do evil an hundred times, and his days be prolonged, yet surely I know that it shall be well with them that fear God, which fear before him:

8:13 But it shall not be well with the wicked, neither shall he prolong his days, which are as a shadow; because he feareth not before God.

The wicked who persecute the zealous for God: shall be destroyed.

> **Matthew 18:6** But whoso shall offend [persecute] one of these little ones **which believe in me**, it were better for him that a millstone were hanged about his neck, and that he were drowned in the depth of the sea.

When the just before God are attacked by the wicked, it is a great evil, and God will not hold the wicked guiltless.

Ecclesiastes 8:14 There is a vanity which is done upon the earth; that there be just men, unto whom it happeneth according to the work of the wicked; again, there be wicked men, to whom it happeneth according to the work of the righteous: I said that this also is vanity.

Solomon advises us to enjoy our lives with propriety and true godliness.

8:15 Then I commended mirth, because a man hath no better thing under the sun, than to eat, and to drink, and to be merry: for that shall abide with him of his labour the days of his life, which God giveth him under the sun.

Solomon considers the works of man and God.

8:16 When I applied mine heart to know wisdom, and to see the business that is done upon the earth: (for also there is [are those] that neither day nor night seeth sleep with his eyes: [but work always] .

The ways of God are far beyond carnal man's understanding:

> **1 Corinthians 2:11** For what man knoweth the things of a man, save the spirit of man which is in him? even so the things of God knoweth no man, but the Spirit of God.

Ecclesiastes 8:17 Then I beheld all the work of God, that a man cannot find out the work that is done under the sun: because though a man labour to seek it out, yet he shall not find it; yea farther; though a wise man think to know it, yet shall he not be able to find it.

Ecclesiastes 9

No man knows the things of God; except those to whom God has given his Holy Spirit of understanding.

Ecclesiastes 9:1 For all this I considered in my heart even to declare all this, that the righteous, and the wise, and their works, are in the hand of God: no man knoweth either love or hatred by all that is before them.

Death is a great evil in the earth.

9:2 All things come alike to all: there is one event to the righteous, and to the wicked; to the good and to the clean, and to the unclean; to him that sacrificeth, and to him that sacrificeth not: as is the good, so is the sinner; and he that sweareth, as he that feareth an oath.

9:3 This is an evil among all things that are done under the sun, that there is one event unto all: yea, also the heart of the sons of men is full of evil, and madness is in their heart while they live, and after that they go to the dead.

9:4 For to him that is joined to all the living there is hope: for a living dog is better than a dead lion.

9:5 For **the living know that they shall die: but the dead know not any thing**, neither have they any more a reward; for the memory of them is forgotten.

9:6 Also their love, and their hatred, and their envy, is now [will perish without repentance] perished; neither have they any more a portion for ever in any thing that is done under the sun.

The faithful to God will be accepted and given the gift of eternal life; therefore be diligent to be faithful to God and to keep ourselves free from the contamination of sin.

Let the called out be diligent to cleave to their espoused Husband and:

9:7 Go thy way, eat thy bread with joy, and drink thy wine with a merry heart; for God now accepteth thy works.

9:8 Let thy garments be always white [let our lives pure free from breaking God's commandments]; and let thy head lack no ointment [a type of God's Spirit].

Instructions for a happy and successful life

9:9 Live joyfully with the wife whom thou lovest all the days of the life of thy vanity, which he hath given thee under the sun, all the days of thy vanity: **for that is thy portion in this life**, and in thy labour which thou takest under the sun.

9:10 Whatsoever thy hand findeth to do, do it with thy might; for there is no work, nor device, nor knowledge, nor wisdom, in the grave, whither thou goest.

9:11 I returned, and saw under the sun, that the race is not to the swift, nor the battle to the strong, neither yet bread to the wise, nor yet riches to men of understanding, nor yet favour to men of skill; but time and chance happeneth to them all.

9:12 For man also knoweth not his time: as the fishes that are taken in an evil net, and as the birds that are caught in the snare; so are the sons of men snared in an evil time, when it falleth suddenly upon them.

The wise words of a poor man are despised, for men look to the great. Men look after the seeing of their eyes, and not according to the wisdom of the spirit of righteousness.

9:13 This wisdom have I seen also under the sun, and it seemed great unto me:

9:14 There was a little city, and few men within it; and there came a great king against it, and besieged it, and built great bulwarks against it:

9:15 Now there was found in it a poor wise man, and he by his wisdom delivered the city; yet no man remembered that same poor man.

9:16 Then said I, Wisdom is better than strength: nevertheless the poor man's wisdom is despised, and his words are not heard.

Wisdom is found in the quiet of prayer and the careful consideration of the words of God; NOT in partying, or in seeking our own ways.

9:17 The words of wise men are heard in quiet more than the cry of him that ruleth among fools.

There is great strength and much good in wisdom; but one sinner can cause much damage; therefore do not allow the openly unconverted in your assemblies.

> **Titus 3:10** A man that is an heretick after the first and second admonition reject; **3:11** Knowing that he that is such is subverted, and sinneth, being condemned of himself.

Ecclesiastes 9:18 Wisdom is better than weapons of war: but one sinner destroyeth much good.

Ecclesiastes 10

Here we begin to come to the conclusion of Solomon; which is that the pursuit of our own ways and of physical things is an empty meaningless struggle which has no lasting value.

It is the things of God which are eternal; and the only value of the present physical life is to learn that following and living by every Word of God is the only thing that has meaning and lasting value.

The next three chapters contain what Solomon has learned in his pursuit of all physical things; which is what the Ekklesia needs to learn today.

In truth our own ways are empty, meaningless, transitory; while eternity, keeping the whole Word of God, is all that really matters. The only value that this physical life has, is as a practical lesson in that truth.

Only a little sin, a little compromise with God's law, teachings and will; causes the otherwise good man to stink in God's nostrils.

Those who teach tolerance of sin for the sake of organizational unity, instead of teaching unity with God through the enthusiastic keeping of

God's commandments are an unclean nauseating odor to God and will be rejected by Christ (Rev 3:16).

Ecclesiastes 10:1 Dead flies cause the ointment of the apothecary to send forth a stinking savour: so doth a little folly him that is in reputation for wisdom and honour.

A wise man will always focus on and look to keep God's commandments with his strong right hand; while the compromising foolish will turn aside out of the ways of God for his heart is not with God.

10:2 A wise man's heart is at his right hand; but a fool's heart at his left.

10:3 Yea also, when he that is a fool walketh by [out of] the way, his [he has no godly wisdom] wisdom faileth him, and he saith to every one that he is a fool.

Do not resist the ruler of all things which is God, by resisting his commandments; for there is no escape from his judgment. When God warns and corrects you repent quickly before him.

10:4 If the spirit of the ruler rise up against thee, leave not thy place; for yielding pacifieth great offences.

It is a great folly for a ruler to teach men to tolerate sin and compromise with God's commandments for organizational unity or for any other purpose. In that organization the spiritually rich in wisdom are brought low and wickedness is exalted above the people.

10:5 There is an evil which I have seen under the sun, as an error [false doctrine] which proceedeth from the ruler:

10:6 Folly [sin] is set in great dignity [by wicked men], and the rich [spiritually rich who are zealous for God and his commandments] sit in low place.

When wickedness rules; the evil are lifted up, while the faithful to God are brought low.

10:7 I have seen servants upon horses, and princes walking as servants upon the earth.

The man who lays snares for the faithful zealous followers of God shall ultimately fall into his own traps and be destroyed in his own pit [the grave].

10:8 He that diggeth a pit shall fall into it; and whoso breaketh an hedge, a serpent shall bite him.

Various Proverbs

10:9 Whoso removeth stones [Physical work can be dangerous but is necessary to prosper] shall be hurt therewith; and he that cleaveth wood shall be endangered thereby.

Think before acting and you will save yourself much labour.

10:10 If the iron [the ax] be blunt, and he do not whet the edge [sharpen the tools], then must he put to more strength: but wisdom is profitable to direct [saving much work].

A person, who spouts out everything they hear and has no discretion, is no better than a serpent lying in wait to bite, for their words of indiscretion will surely bite many.

10:11 Surely the serpent will bite without enchantment; and a babbler is no better.

A wise man will speak wise things, teaching the wisdom of God's commandments; but a foolish man will teach foolish rebellion against zeal for God's commandments, that may appear wise to worldly men, but is foolishness just the same.

10:12 The words of a wise man's mouth are gracious; but the lips of a fool will swallow up himself.

10:13 The beginning of the words of [the compromiser with God's law] his mouth is foolishness: and the end of his talk is mischievous madness.

The wicked often bury their false doctrine in a multitude of words.

10:14 A fool also is full of words: a man cannot tell what shall be; and what shall be after him, who can tell him?

10:15 The labour of the foolish wearieth every one of them, because he knoweth not how to go to the city [of God, the temple of God and God's gift of life eternal].

10:16 Woe to thee, O land, when thy king is a [ignorant and lacking knowledge like a] child, and thy princes [leaders feed themselves first] eat in the morning!

10:17 Blessed art thou, O land, when thy king is the son of nobles [When the king is the son of righteous and Godly wise advisors], and thy princes eat [feed the people and take only what is appropriate for themselves and not to make themselves intoxicated with wealth or worldly pleasures: and in the spiritual sense feed on God's Word] in due season, for strength, and not for drunkenness!

We have been lax, lukewarm and slothful about our spiritual house and we have had a misguided zeal for the physical.

10:18 By much slothfulness the building decayeth; and through idleness of the hands the house droppeth [collapses] through.

One cannot feast or drink wine without wealth. Therefore let us lay up spiritual wealth that we may rejoice in our God.

10:19 A feast is made for laughter, and wine maketh merry: but money answereth all things.

God knows all our heart and he knows the thoughts of our minds. Therefore discipline your very nature to zealously keep all of God's commandments and internalize them as a part of our very natures.

10:20 Curse not the king, no not in thy thought; and curse not the rich in thy bedchamber: for a bird of the air shall carry the voice, and that which hath wings shall tell the matter.

Ecclesiastes 11

If we are generous to others we shall make friends and have our reward from God

Ecclesiastes 11:1 Cast thy bread upon the waters: for thou shalt find it after many days.

11:2 Give a portion to seven, and also to eight; for thou knowest not what evil shall be upon the earth.

Be generous to others as God is generous to us, but give out of our blessings, and do not give what we do not have. Also give unto those who have claims on us; providing what is needed to our families and creditors.

When we give to the needy [BOTH physically and the spiritual gifts of teaching God's truth], and obey God; then in due time God will give to us spiritual riches and eternal life; therefore the gift really remains with us as the fallen tree remains in its place.

11:3 If the clouds be full of rain, they empty themselves upon the earth: and if the tree fall toward the south, or toward the north, in the place where the tree falleth, there it shall be.

The lazy man [physically or spiritually] who will not put effort into his work; shall not reap physical or spiritual gain

> **Matthew 25:24** Then he which had received the one talent came and said, Lord, I knew thee that thou art an hard man, reaping where thou hast not sown, and gathering where thou hast not strawed: **25:25** And I was afraid, and went and hid thy talent in the earth: lo, there thou hast that is thine.
>
> **25:26** His lord answered and said unto him, Thou wicked and slothful servant, thou knewest that I reap where I sowed not, and gather where I have not strawed: **25:27** Thou oughtest therefore to have put my money to the exchangers, and then at my coming I should have received mine own with usury.
>
> **25:28** Take therefore the talent from him, and give it unto him which hath ten talents.
>
> **25:29** For unto every one that hath shall be given, and he shall have abundance: but from him that hath not shall be taken away even that which he hath. **25:30** And cast ye the unprofitable servant into outer darkness: there shall be weeping and gnashing of teeth.

Brethren, we have been deceived and distracted into doing a business

Brethren, I tell you the truth. Unless we become zealous to live by every Word of God and to study to learn and grow in repentance and knowledge; we shall NOT be in the resurrection of first fruits.

Ecclesiastes 11:4 He that observeth the wind shall not sow; and he that regardeth the clouds shall not reap.

Man with the spirit of a man, knows nothing of God. It is only by the Spirit of God, given to those who commit to obeying God; that godly things are understood.

11:5 As thou knowest not what is the way of the spirit, nor how the bones do grow in the womb of her that is with child: even so thou knowest not the works of God who maketh all.

Work night and day as David did [Psalm 119] to seek out God and learn of God's ways to zealously keep them.

11:6 In the morning sow thy seed, and in the evening withhold not thine hand: for thou knowest not whether shall prosper, either this or that, or whether they both shall be alike good.

The light [scriptures and law] of God is sweet to convert the soul; just remember the days of darkness from which God's Word has liberated us, so that we do not return to spiritual Egypt.

11:7 Truly the light is sweet, and a pleasant thing it is for the eyes to behold the sun:

11:8 But if a man live many years, and rejoice in them all; yet let him remember the days of darkness; for they shall be many. All that cometh is vanity.

Live life to the full according to the commandments of God; for we shall all be judged by the same God, out of the same books; according to our works.

> **Revelation 20:12** And I saw the dead, small and great, stand before God; and the books were opened: and another book was opened, which is the book of life: and the dead were judged out of those things which were written in the books, according to their works.

Ecclesiastes 11:9 Rejoice, O young man, in thy youth; and let thy heart cheer thee in the days of thy youth, and walk in the ways of thine heart, and in the sight of thine eyes: but know thou, that for all these things God will bring thee into judgment.

Put away the evil and excess of youth and learn of God to zealously keep all of his commandments.

11:10 Therefore remove sorrow from thy heart, and put away evil from thy flesh: for childhood and youth are vanity.

Ecclesiastes 12

Remember God and his law in our youth; before we are old and our eyes be dimmed and there is no more pleasure in life

Ecclesiastes 12:1 Remember now thy Creator in the days of thy youth, while the evil days come not, nor the years draw nigh, when thou shalt say, I have no pleasure in them;

12:2 While the sun, or the light, or the moon, or the stars, be not darkened, nor the clouds return after the rain:

12:3 In the day when [death approaches] the keepers of the house shall tremble, and the strong men shall bow themselves, and the grinders cease because they are few and those that look out of the windows be darkened, [eyesight is] be darkened,

12:4 And the doors shall be shut in the streets, when the sound of the grinding is low, and he shall rise up at the voice of the bird, and all the daughters of musick shall be brought low;

12:5 Also when they shall be afraid of that which is high, and fears shall be in the way, and the almond tree shall flourish, and the grasshopper shall be a burden, and desire shall fail: because man goeth to his long home [of the grave], and the mourners go about the streets:

12:6 Or ever the silver cord be loosed, or the golden bowl be broken, or the pitcher be broken at the fountain, or the wheel broken at the cistern.

The spirits of the dead return to God to be kept in his care for the resurrections; when they shall be placed in new bodies.

12:7 Then shall the [people] dust return to the earth as it was: and the spirit shall return unto God who gave it.

12:8 Vanity of vanities, saith the preacher; all is vanity.

Even though Solomon was vexed with the vanity of physical life, he still taught the people in many Proverbs. This seems to indicate that the proverbs may have been written after Ecclesiastes.

12:9 And moreover, because the preacher was wise, he still taught the people knowledge; yea, he gave good heed, and sought out, and set in order many proverbs.

12:10 The preacher sought to find out acceptable words: and that which was written was upright, even words of truth.

12:11 The words of the wise are as goads [to do the righteousness of God's commandments], and as nails fastened by the masters of assemblies, which are given from one shepherd.

The study of physical things is endless; the things of real value are the things of God.

12:12 And further, by these, my son, be admonished: of making many books there is no end; and much study is a weariness of the flesh.

12:13 Let us hear the conclusion of the whole matter: Fear God, and keep his commandments: for this is the whole duty of man.

12:14 For God shall bring every work into judgment, with every secret thing, whether it be good, or whether it be evil.

Visit Our Website

theshininglight.info

www.ingramcontent.com/pod-product-compliance
Lightning Source LLC
Chambersburg PA
CBHW081938170426
43202CB00018B/2942